THE ART OF
THORNTON WILDER

THE ART OF
THORNTON WILDER

by Malcolm Goldstein

UNIVERSITY OF NEBRASKA PRESS · LINCOLN

Acknowledgments for the use of copyrighted material
appear on pages 175–176.

Publishers on the Plains

UNP

Library of Congress Catalog Card Number 65–10239

Manufactured in the United States of America

To Ralph and Ann Clark

Contents

Foreword

THIS BRIEF STUDY of the literary career of Thornton Wilder is an attempt to reach three goals. Lest the reader expect it to be what it is not, I wish to describe the goals at the outset.

First, I hope that the book is a readable and useful guide to Wilder's plays and novels. To this end, I have taken up each in its chronological position, have commented on the specific literary sources of each, and have investigated the ideas underlying Wilder's writing in its entirety. If I have succeeded, the reader will recognize the continuity of the author's thought from his publications of half a century ago to the present. Like most writers, Wilder employs a single theme repeatedly, but, as I have tried to demonstrate, he is superior to most in the invention of fresh modes of expression, each appropriate to the theme, and each capable of creating and sustaining the emotional force necessary for its acceptance.

Second, I hope I have communicated my own pleasure in Wilder's writing. I will not deny my reservations about the early novels, many of the short dramatic sketches, and one of the Broadway plays, but behind all my remarks is the long-standing conviction that Wilder is a major writer. He has never been neglected, it is true, but he has less often received serious attention outside the classroom than have his contemporaries of comparable reputation. I should especially like to extend his readership to include all who without looking at his work have shrugged it off as sentimental or pedantic. It is neither.

The third purpose of the book is to provide such biographical material as will enhance our understanding of the work itself. It is a paradox that this least secretive, most gregarious of authors wishes not to be the subject of a full-scale biography during his own lifetime. He has long been helpful to students of his work and has cordially answered queries from high school pupils, members of graduate seminars, and professional critics, but has drawn the line at detailed questions concerning persons and places. Nevertheless, so frequently have accounts of his travels, public appearances, and social engagements appeared in the press that it is no very difficult task to piece together a view of the whole man. Miss Isabel Wilder, the writer's sister, has shown great patience with my requests for information on Wilder's non-literary activities beyond what is available in newspapers and magazines. During his withdrawal to the Arizona desert to write in freedom from just such requests, she relayed to him those few questions which she herself was unable to answer. I hope that I have accurately reported the facts she has supplied. The reader will discover the extent to which I am in her debt through the frequent appearance of her name in the notes. It is a pleasure to make a more precise acknowledgment here.

I should also like to thank three friends who had the kindness to hear me out on many matters related to the book. They are Professor Lillian Feder, Mr. William Guthrie, and Mrs. Donald Symington.

THE ART OF
THORNTON WILDER

I. Outline of a Life

IN THE COUNTRYSIDE near Rome on a day in the academic year 1920–1921 the young Thornton Niven Wilder came upon a scene so far beyond the range of his usual experience and yet so gripping that the ideas it evoked have never ceased, in nearly half a century since the event, to demand exploration in his fiction and drama. It was, as he has described it, the consequence of a quite ordinary physical act: shoveling up the earth in an archaeological excavation. But the sight of the long-buried Etruscan street which he himself helped to uncover left him "never the same again." [1] Here was the evidence that the past is a sustaining force in present life and that the present itself is only a segment of an endless continuum. No matter how simply it is phrased, this idea is anything but simple, and in his few comments on the origin of his literary career Wilder has never slighted its importance. Moreover, hints of his awareness of the stream of history appear in even the brief stories and plays which he published before his visit to Rome, as though the idea had awaited one startling impulse to give it full form in his mind.

[1] Wilder, "Joyce and the Modern Novel," in *A James Joyce Miscellany*, ed. Marvin Magalaner (n.p.: James Joyce Society, 1957), pp. 13–14.

Once lifted to the level of his conscious thought, the concept of eternity as all-important to the activities of man became Wilder's principal literary theme. To anyone less observant of the world around him than he himself has always been, a sense of the relative insignificance of the here and now when viewed within the context of eternity might carry with it a loss of esteem for individual life. But to Wilder it has brought a sympathetic understanding of man as a creature so bewildered by the speed with which his short span passes into history that, far from making the most of it, he is numb to its opportunities. On the one hand, any man is foolish to claim much for his own feelings and experiences when they are measured against those of all humanity, past and present. But on the other, he is no less unwise to live without fully relishing whatever life brings to him, and at the moment of its arrival, since he can never re-experience an emotion or repeat an action.

The conditions of his life from childhood onward had prepared Wilder for the revelation in Italy. After his graduation from Yale in 1920 he had gone to Rome on a fellowship offered by the American Academy in that city. It was his first trip to Europe, but not his first trip abroad. Born in Madison, Wisconsin, on April 17, 1897, the surviving member of a set of twins, he was still a young boy when the family left the Midwest to move on across the continent and out to Hong Kong, where his father, Amos P. Wilder, was to serve as American Consul General from 1906 to 1909. Thornton spent only six months of 1906 in the Orient before his father sent him and his mother, brother, and two sisters[2] back to America, but this brief period was eventful. His everyday life in the alien culture of Hong Kong, astonishing enough in itself, was complicated further by his attendance at a German-

[2] Later a third daughter was born to the family.

language school in the city. On returning to the States, Mrs. Wilder and her children took up residence, not in Madison, but in another and quite different university town: Berkeley, California. In 1911 they went again to China. Mr. Wilder was then serving in Shanghai, where for a few weeks Thornton was enrolled in another German school before going off to the English China Inland Mission School at Chefoo. Back in California once more in 1913, Thornton went first to the Thacher School in Ojai and then to Berkeley High School, from which he graduated in 1915. Such settlements, voyages, and re-settlements as Wilder made in those early years are not especially remarkable for numbers alone. They come a long way, however, toward explaining the feeling for the vastness of space and time and the fascination with distant cultures observable throughout his literary career, as well as the absence of interest in American life which marks his apprentice work and the products of his first ten years as a professional writer. And by exposing him to modes of life far different from those sanctioned by the strict Calvinism of his family, they helped to develop the imagination which at the beginning of the 1920's peopled a Roman ditch with ancient Etruscans.

Within the family circle it was Thornton's mother, the former Isabella Thornton Niven, who most encouraged his intellectual growth. His father's role was chiefly that of disciplinarian. Before entering the diplomatic service, Amos P. Wilder had studied at Yale and, after graduation, had worked as a newspaperman. Although it might be supposed that exposure to New Haven, various editorial offices, and diplomacy would leave him broadly receptive to life, he was never moved to break out of the slim channels of asceticism of the Congregational Church in which he had been raised. Mrs. Wilder was brought up in Presbyterianism, a sect no more disposed toward worldliness than her husband's, but she was given to a strong desire to learn and did not fear that an active intellectual life would weaken her devotion. In Berkeley she found opportunities to study informally by attending lectures at the University of California and by participating in foreign-language discussion groups. She was fully aware that her husband, were he present, would not approve, but she encouraged her children, nevertheless, in their independent, extracurricular search for knowledge. Her spirit is detectable in the careers of her elder son, Amos, a theologian who has written poetry and literary criticism, and her second daughter, Isabel, who is the author of three novels, as well as in her younger son's work. It is clear that as a boy Thornton felt the pull between father and mother; as late as 1935, in the novel *Heaven's My Destination*, he created out of memories of his father, his brother, and himself when young a comic hero who is never to shake off the restraints of Calvinism.[3]

In 1915 the senior Wilder won a kind of victory when at his insistence Thornton set off for Oberlin College in Ohio rather than for Yale, which he would have preferred. Yale, according to the father, was worldly and therefore dangerous; having studied there himself, he was convinced it would not do for his son, whereas the small, quiet, midwestern campus would provide proper spiritual enrichment. Two years later, however, Thornton transferred to Yale, and with Amos P. Wilder's resignation from the Consular Service, the entire family settled in New Haven. This was the time of the First World War, and Thornton, eager to enlist, interrupted his education for eight months of duty with the Coast Artillery, the only branch of the services that did not turn him down for poor eyesight. In 1919 he returned to Yale for his senior year, grateful, despite his affection for the university, to have had

[3] Biographical details supplied by Miss Isabel Wilder.

a change of scene, even though he had gone no farther away than Fort Adams, Rhode Island.[4] If the family's influence on his personality held on stubbornly, at least he had begun to free himself, however gradually, of controls on his actions.

Meanwhile Wilder had begun to write, and to publish. As early as his year at Thacher he had developed the practice of filling up spare hours and the duller moments of class periods in literary creativity. In his first term at Oberlin he found a suitable outlet in the college literary journal; in the two Ohio years he brought out nine pieces. At Yale he increased his productivity and served on the staff of the *Literary Magazine*. In all, he had published thirty-two short works by the time of his graduation, including four in the new and curiously named "little" magazine, *S4N*. The few poems and reviews among the undergraduate writings are very brief, but the plays and stories which make up the bulk of this body of work are slightly more extended and decidedly polished. The frequency of their appearance gives evidence, not of precocity, since Wilder was slightly older than the average college student, but of a deepening determination to examine all the varieties of literary form. Drama, however, is the preferred genre: over half are plays, of which most are supposed to require no more than three minutes in production. But the writings also include one long, elaborate allegory in four acts.

Although his mother's speculative mind was an early influence of undoubtable importance, other forces in his boyhood and youth contributed much to Wilder's first writings and extended their pressures when he took up a career as a professional man of letters. The fondness for

[4] Richard H. Goldstone, "Thornton Wilder," in *Writers at Work: The Paris Review Interviews*, ed. Malcolm Cowley (New York: Viking Press, 1958), p. 103; Isabel Wilder.

drama came upon him in his school days and remained to bring about, in time, the works for which he is most likely to be remembered. As early as his adolescence Wilder frequented the stock plays and road shows at Ye Liberty Theatre in Oakland[5] and kept abreast, as best he could in the comparative isolation of the West in his boyhood, of new currents in drama. For the most part Oakland offered romances and rough farces; Edward Peple's *The Prince Chap*, Edwin Milton Doyle's *The Straw Man*, and David Belasco's *Rose of the Rancho* are a few which Ye Liberty advertised in the Oakland *Tribune* in Wilder's day. But the literary drama of Europe, especially as produced by Max Reinhardt in Berlin and Vienna, offered substantial matter to read and think about, if not to see, and from a distance of six thousand miles Wilder kept up with late developments. It is no wonder that Wilder's first dramatic efforts are high-flown.

At Oberlin Wilder was fortunate in finding at least one very sympathetic teacher: Charles Wager, whose passion for literature made him something of a classroom spellbinder. It was probably as a result of Wager's enthusiastic performances, which ranged beyond his field of nineteenth-century English literature to include the great writers of antiquity and the Renaissance, that Wilder developed a taste for comparativist studies. If the first pieces written at Oberlin share any qualities with the work of the mature writer, it is a sense of the cumulative process in literary history: a conviction that it is reasonable and indeed inevitable for the writer to take what is valuable from his predecessors for the development of his own work and that national boundaries are of no importance in literary study. "Every great work," according to Wager, "was written this morning";[6] the quality of greatness in

[5] Wilder, *Three Plays* (New York: Harper & Brothers, 1957), p. xiii.
[6] "An Obliging Man," *Time*, LXI (Jan. 12, 1953), 45.

literature is the ability of a work to sustain its effect throughout history, to keep its freshness.

Wager's classes, with their emphasis on the great, proven works, were Wilder's introduction to the new humanistic school of criticism. In the first decades of the century, under the leadership of Paul Elmer More of Princeton and Irving Babbitt of Harvard, humanism became the primary approach to literature at the universities. Impatient with the microscopic naturalism of twentieth-century American literature, which struck them as evidence of moral decay, these philosopher-critics urged upon the academic intelligentsia an attitude of Christian forbearance and optimism. In this was implicit an aristocratic refusal to concern themselves deeply with those aspects of life which may be described as squalid, unhealthy, or unharmonious. Submission to the authority of the Christian Church, which would induce a sense of moral values, was their solution to mankind's problems, not an intense analysis, in the fashion of the naturalists, of the antagonistic forces in society which created the problems. Understandably, Wilder responded affirmatively to humanistic thought. Protected by father and mother alike from contact with physical and emotional squalor, prepared by the family faith to accept self-discipline as a moral necessity, he was not inclined to emulate the naturalists' investigations of earthiness or to bring into his writing their calculated coarseness. His three novels of the 1920's, Wilder's first major works as a professional man of letters, demonstrate the very strong attraction of humanism to him. It was inevitable that, if he should write at all, he should write in full consciousness of the academic attitudes into which his studies and natural bent had taken him, but it was unfortunate that the appearance in print of the novels should coincide with the severe repudiation of humanism on the part of non-academic, chiefly radical, critics. Of the three, only *The Bridge of San Luis Rey* possessed the strength to survive the change of taste.

From his graduation until 1928 Wilder remained in academic life while continuing to write. The fellowship at the American Academy which he won during his senior year did not require him to study formally for an advanced degree; he worked at the diggings, but had no plan of continuing in archaeology. On hearing that his father had secured a job for him as a teacher of French, he came home at the end of the year in Rome. The position was offered by the Lawrenceville School, a preparatory school of great distinction situated in the pleasant country between Trenton and Princeton, New Jersey. In addition to his classroom work, Wilder also had the duties of an assistant housemaster; eventually he became master of Davis House at the school. He remained in New Jersey for seven years, with summer interludes of travel. From 1924 to 1926 he withdrew from the school to take the M.A. degree in French from Princeton, and when the success of his second novel, *The Bridge of San Luis Rey*, gave him financial independence, he resigned from the school altogether.

The rare beauty and placidity of the neighboring communities of Lawrenceville and Princeton are all but irresistible to men of contemplative mind. In the 1920's, before heavy industry had begun to dispatch freight trucks through the roads of both towns, and before the towns themselves had become the havens of minor business executives employed in New York and Philadelphia, the school and the university came as close to embodying the popular notion of the ivory tower as such institutions can ever come. In the first decade of the century a rancorous dispute between Woodrow Wilson, then President of Princeton, and Andrew Fleming West, the graduate dean,

over the site of Princeton's new Graduate College had
ended with victory for West and the construction of the
College on ground near but not adjoining the main campus. Ever since, the graduate students have had to endure
the inconvenience of a fifteen-minute walk from their
rooms to the library and laboratories, but for compensation
they have had the benefit of quiet on their return, as well
as a valuable sense of remoteness from undergraduate
frivolity. But a graduate college is not a monastery, and
graduate students give up no worldly pleasures; it is in
certain ways instructive to note that during Prohibition
a speakeasy flourished not more than half a mile from the
graduate buildings at Princeton. Taken all in all, including
the speakeasy, it was a superbly comfortable area in
which to spend seven years—at least for a man who, like
Wilder, is both studious and convivial.

These years formed a remarkably busy, productive
period in Wilder's life. He helped to edit *S4N* and continued to submit short pieces to the magazine until its
demise in 1925. During the summer of that year he made
the first of many visits to the MacDowell Colony in
Peterborough, New Hampshire. There, in the encamp-
ment designed for the encouragement of the arts, he could
enjoy a mountain climate which contrasted in its coolness
with the humid stuffiness of the New Jersey summer.
(Wilder has long remembered a cheerful chauffeur who
used to remark as colonists set out for a drive, "There goes
ten tons of talent." [7]) In the spring of 1926 came his first
novel, *The Cabala*; in the fall of the same year, a production
at the American Repertory Theatre in New York, of his
full-length undergraduate play, *The Trumpet Shall Sound*;
in the fall of 1927, *The Bridge of San Luis Rey*; and in the
fall of 1928, a collection of his three-minute sketches, *The
Angel That Troubled the Waters and Other Plays*. Concerning

[7] Isabel Wilder.

these last pieces he has said that some were composed at Lawrenceville "after the lights of the House were
out and the sheaf of absurd French exercises corrected
and indignantly marked with red crayon." [8] These were
the conditions under which he wrote the novels as well;
to the boys whose rooms were below his study, the sound
of his pacing was the clue that another work was in progress.[9] The mere sight of the handsome academic buildings in which he spent these years has anaesthetized some
would-be scholars and writers, even to the point of rendering them too weak to move away. Wilder, however,
enjoyed himself, served the school well, wrote his novels
and dramatic sketches, and escaped, his powers as strong
as in the year of his arrival.

It was an almost totally different world that Wilder
entered on his departure from Lawrenceville. The tepid
reception of *The Cabala*, his novel of modern Roman
society, provided no preparation for the immense popularity of his novel of eighteenth-century Peru, *The Bridge
of San Luis Rey*. This romantic, low-keyed depiction of the
lives of Spanish colonials became a best-seller immediately
on its publication; in the first twelve months it sold
300,000 copies.[10] New printings of *The Cabala* became
necessary, and, as another result, the volume of three-
minute plays was published. At the peak of the clamor over
the novel, it was awarded the Pulitzer Prize in May 1928,
the first of three such prizes Wilder has received. Although
he had never experienced financial difficulties, he had not
before this time known such freedom as his royalties made
possible. Conditioned to the enjoyment of travel from
boyhood, he set out for Europe. With his sister Isabel he

[8] Wilder, *The Angel That Troubled the Waters and Other Plays in One Act*
(New York: Coward-McCann, 1928), p. xiii.

[9] "An Obliging Man," 45.

[10] Malcolm Cowley, introduction, *A Thornton Wilder Trio* (New York:
Criterion Books, 1956), p. 4.

visited Vienna and Berlin, reporting on drama for *Theatre Arts Monthly*. Abroad he was lionized as steadily as at home; such eminent members of the literary world as André Maurois and Bernard Shaw welcomed him. He stayed for a while in Paris and met Sylvia Beach, the imaginative American bookseller who published James Joyce's *Ulysses*. (Later Miss Beach wrote with regret that in the 1930's Wilder drifted out of the circle of her acquaintance after coming to know Gertrude Stein, with whom she was not on good terms.[11]) Somewhat astonishingly, he became a good friend of Gene Tunney, the heavyweight boxing champion who had caused heads to wag in both the literary and sporting worlds by the announcement that he was giving up the ring to read Shakespeare; in 1928 Wilder and Tunney made a walking tour of the Rhine Valley, and true to his avowed intention, Tunney took along a copy of *King Lear*.[12] Returning to America, Wilder visited Scott and Zelda Fitzgerald in their home near Wilmington, and there he met Edmund Wilson.[13] And in addition to all this evidence of fame was the construction in 1930 of a comfortable wood and stone hillside house in Hamden, Connecticut, outside New Haven, where he could rest when the rambles ended. Appropriately, Wilder nicknamed it "the house *The Bridge* built."

Despite the frequency of his travels and the increasing tempo of his social activities, Wilder found time to write. In 1930 he published a third novel, *The Woman of Andros*, and in the following year, a collection of six short plays somewhat cumbersomely titled *The Long Christmas Dinner*

[11] Sylvia Beach, *Shakespeare and Company* (New York: Harcourt, Brace, 1959), p. 111.

[12] Glenway Wescott, *Images of Truth* (New York: Harper & Row, 1962), p. 255.

[13] Edmund Wilson, *The Shores of Light* (New York: Farrar, Straus and Young, 1952), pp. 375–383.

and Other Plays in One Act. The novel, a torpid, small-compassed romance of the Greek islands in antiquity, proved a sharp disappointment to his readers; no appeals to the memory of *The Bridge* could drive the tediousness from the language or lend allure to the unfortunately quaint setting. But if Wilder's fiction was generally ignored in the bookshops, it received the careful attention of his fellow-writers, as the result of a sensationally harsh review in the *New Republic*. For two months at the close of the year the defects and merits of this and Wilder's three earlier books were weighed in the correspondence columns of the magazine, while the novelist himself remained silent. The publication of the new volume of plays one year later came as something of an anticlimax.

Wilder's taciturnity in the face of this controversy is a reminder of the lesson learned at the Roman diggings. He had begun, it would seem, to demonstrate in his personal life an awareness of the flow of time and the danger inherent in fixing oneself on a solitary issue. To brood over criticism of his writing would have bound him intellectually to work already accomplished; by ignoring the review and its aftermath he minimized a serious threat to his growth, as well as a threat to the continued enjoyment of the pleasures his productivity had earned for him. Now, having accepted a new academic post for the fall of 1930, he took up his duties enthusiastically.

The position was a lectureship in comparative literature at the University of Chicago. The offer made to Wilder was especially advantageous, inasmuch as it left him with considerable freedom for writing—he was to give classes during only half the academic year. Alternating his periods of teaching with work on the book of plays, a translation, and a novel, he continued at the post through the spring of 1936. He managed the time also for two cross-country lecture tours, a term as visiting professor at the University of Hawaii, short stretches of screen-writing in Hollywood (but without screen credits), and the usual transatlantic wandering. These were years of amazing acceleration during which Wilder no sooner arrived anywhere than he seemed to be departing. Yet they were also productive years; the quality of the books published in 1931 and 1935 reveals a development in his skill as a writer to match his flamboyant indulgence in all the other, seemingly irresistible activities.

At Chicago he entered a different sort of academic routine from what he had known at Lawrenceville, where the task of the teacher requires not instruction alone, but, as in all preparatory schools, the supervision of the boys' daily life. In the 1930's, under the administration of the young Robert Maynard Hutchins, Wilder's onetime co-worker on the Yale *Lit*, Chicago differed also from the two older universities at which he had taken his degrees. As a physical plant, to be sure, with its long Midway edged by neo-Gothic buildings in the best Eastern collegiate style, it resembled Yale or Princeton closely enough to make an alumnus of those institutions feel quite at home. But this was no more than a superficial likeness. Ignoring the gradual deterioration of the once-fashionable neighborhood in which it had been constructed in the 1890's, the university had rapidly established itself as an intellectual center, and with Hutchins, only thirty on his appointment as president in 1929, it was making a radical attempt to alter the American undergraduate system by admitting well-trained high school students at the end of their sophomore year. One result of this program was the development of a young student body notable for priding itself on its lack of the customary undergraduate zeal for Alma Mater as a purely social environment. There were, however, the usual outlets for the convivial natures university professors and students are likely to possess. Wilder is said never to have failed to answer the taps on the door of his apartment and often to have gone out for an evening's spree in the Loop with his students.

In the Chicago years began Wilder's close friendship with Gertrude Stein, an association of great value to the lives of both writers. The first meeting of the two occurred when Miss Stein made a visit to America from October 1934 to May 1935, the only return to her native country she was to make after 1903, the year of her settlement in Europe. That the two had not met in Paris on Wilder's trips abroad in the 1920's is something of a distinction, if a peculiar one, on his part. Almost alone among the young American writers then passing through the city, he had felt no inclination to join the circle of expatriates whom the gregarious Miss Stein entertained and lectured in her rooms in the rue de Fleurus. It is a distinction also that Wilder was one of the few friends with whom she never bickered; from the moment of their first encounter until the outbreak of the Second World War, when communication between them became impossible, they remained on close footing. An invitation to deliver a series of lectures to her compatriots was the lure which brought Miss Stein out of her exile. The tour which she undertook in America led her to the campuses of most major universities and colleges, and at each she delighted her audiences by displaying a degree of wit and candor seldom detectable in her prose. In November she stopped, along with her ever-present companion, Alice Toklas, at the University of Chicago, where her talk on "Poetry and Grammar" (published in 1935 as the sixth of her *Lectures in America*) before an audience of five hundred so impressed President Hutchins that he invited her to return in the early spring, after the conclusion of her tour.[14]

For their second stay at the university, Wilder lent the two ladies his apartment, and the friendship was secure. He was no less charmed by Miss Stein than were the crowds of curiosity-seekers who came to look at her during her *wanderjahr*. As the years passed, he became one of the strongest props of her literary reputation; ultimately, and with unchecked admiration, he was to provide introductions to three of her books: *Narration*, the set of lectures written especially for the University of Chicago; *The Geographical History of America, or The Relation of Human Nature to the Human Mind*, a work for which she requested in vain that he provide running marginal commentaries; and the posthumously published *Four in America*. For each book his praise is so unstinting as to pique the curiosity of all but the steadiest anti-Steinians. During the fall of 1935 Wilder visited her and Miss Toklas at their summer home in Bilignin, where he worked on the manuscripts of new plays; other visits occurred in 1937 and 1939. Miss Stein found *Heaven's My Destination*, Wilder's fourth novel, an excellent interpretation of American life (an opinion which she also held of Harry Leon Wilson's *Merton of the Movies*), unlike Sigmund Freud, who, Wilder confided to her, had dismissed the book with a few blunt words. On reading the *Geographical History* in manuscript shortly after his first visit to Bilignin, Wilder offered a compliment in return for hers: the book, and

[14] On the Stein-Wilder friendship as reported in this and the following paragraph, see Gertrude Stein, *Everybody's Autobiography* (New York: Random House, 1937), p. 261; John Malcolm Brinnin, *The Third Rose, Gertrude Stein and Her World* (Boston: Little, Brown, 1959), pp. 337–338, 353, 359; Donald Gallup ed., *The Flowers of Friendship: Letters to Gertrude Stein* (New York: Alfred A. Knopf, 1953), p. 336.

"what a book," was to his mind "absorbing and fascinating and fantastically gay."[15] In 1938 with the production of *Our Town*, Wilder's masterwork of the decade, came the greatest compliment, for the play gave new shape to the ideas of American life and the American mind which Gertrude Stein had expounded in the long manuscript and in her university lectures.

Gradually through the 1930's Wilder turned his energies away from fiction toward the theater. His ever-widening circle of friends began to include persons of eminence in all the theatrical crafts, and inevitably the friendships led to collaboration. Wilder got his first taste of the professional theater in 1932, when he translated André Obey's *The Rape of Lucrece* for Katharine Cornell. The production was a failure, but it took his name to Broadway. Alexander Woollcott, whose prestige as critic and wit was then immense, became his intimate; he became a frequent guest at the river island in Vermont where Woollcott operated a small-scale resort for friends. Edward Sheldon, the blind, paralyzed author of *Salvation Nell* and *Romance*, among other plays, also befriended him, and Wilder entered the group of distinguished performers and writers who accepted, and profited from, Sheldon's advice on their work. Jed Harris, the irascible, brash *enfant terrible* among Broadway producers, was still another new friend. Looking for a suitable starring vehicle for the versatile actress Ruth Gordon, the two planned that Wilder should make a fresh translation of Ibsen's *A Doll's House*.[16] Produced and directed by Harris, this work opened on Broadway late in 1937. Less than two months later, Harris staged the play which climaxed Wilder's activity of the 1930's: *Our Town*.

[15] Wilder to Gertrude Stein, Oct. 7, 1935, in Gallup, pp. 305–307.
[16] Isabel Wilder.

With this production, Wilder's career underwent a sharp change in both its direction and its very tone. The play not only strengthened the reputation which had begun to sag with the failures of *The Woman of Andros* and *Heaven's My Destination*; it revealed one of the very few native American talents of the first rank in drama. Although Wilder's two collections of one-act pieces, *The Trumpet Shall Sound*, and the translations had all been noted in the press, he had gained recognition not through these efforts, but through his fiction. Now, however, he became known principally as a dramatist, and the novels fell into profound neglect. In retrospect, *Heaven's My Destination*, his novel of the Great Depression, appears by virtue of its glimpses of the national poverty and desuetude to be Wilder's response to the anti-humanist critics who had reproached him for ignoring his own country in the novels of the 1920's. Even so, it did not appease them, and they were not to be moved to a reconsideration after the successful opening of *Our Town*. The play, on the other hand, caught the mood of the period brilliantly. Set in New England near the beginning of the century, it gave theatergoers the flavor of a gentler, less feverish age—something they very much wanted— and comforted them with its peculiarly American atmosphere at a time when Europe was seething with rearmament. Since the entire spectrum of political opinion from far-right isolationism to far-left interventionism wished to encourage representations of "grass-roots America" in the arts, the play won general favor. In all quarters the award to Wilder of the Pulitzer Prize for this play met with approval. It was assumed that he would continue to make impressive contributions to the theater.

In the wake of the good notices came a renewal of interest in Wilder's personal life. Not since *The Bridge of San Luis Rey* had he been so frequently photographed, interviewed, consulted. So small a matter as his taking a lease on a New York apartment became copy for the press.[17] Excellent business for *Our Town* was assured for the two weeks in September 1938 when, in his first and only appearance as a Broadway actor, Wilder substituted for Frank Craven in the central role of the Stage Manager. In the following year, becoming a star of the summer circuit, he played the part in Cohasset, Dennis, and Stockbridge, Massachusetts. One of the problems of acting, he then discovered, was the work of memorizing his own lines.[18]

The public expectations were at least partially fulfilled by Wilder's work of the next few years. *The Merchant of Yonkers*, his second Broadway play, opened late in 1938 for a brief run. By securing Max Reinhardt, whom he had long admired, to stage the play, Wilder fulfilled an old ambition, only to see the Viennese director render heavy and dull what should have been a wildly spinning farce. The early closing may have been disappointing, but it apparently was not flattening; he was soon back at work. To a reporter sent to interview him between performances of *Our Town* on Cape Cod, he said nothing of his plans, but remarked that he was studying James Joyce's *Finnegans Wake*,[19] a book so recently published that among general readers very little was known of it beyond the fact of its extraordinary complexity. Three years were to pass before he gave form to his speculations on the *Wake* in his third Broadway play, *The Skin of Our Teeth*. In the interim he worked at another play, to be called *The Emporium*; many rumors circulated in the press during 1940 and

[17] "Thornton Wilder Signs for a Suite," New York *Times*, Nov. 9, 1939, p. 43.

[18] "News of the Stage," New York *Times*, Sept. 14, 1938, p. 26; John Franchey, "Mr. Wilder Has an Idea," New York *Times*, Aug. 13, 1939, Sec. IX, p. 2.

[19] Franchey, *loc. cit.*

1941 that this piece was to be produced on Broadway, but Wilder could not convince himself of its merit and has never authorized a production.

Wilder had already slipped into middle age when Europe went to war in 1939 and by the time of Pearl Harbor he was close to forty-five. Although he might have honorably spared himself the rigors of participation in the war by virtue of his age, characteristically he committed himself to a most active role. In mid-1941, as America strengthened her relations with her natural allies, he made two trips abroad: first a State Department tour of South America, where he was widely respected as the author of *The Bridge of San Luis Rey*, and then a visit to England, in the worst of the blitz, as a guest of the British government and a delegate, along with John Dos Passos, to the International P.E.N., where as the moment required he spoke on the invincibility of the democracies. After America's inevitable declaration of war, he waited only a few months before planning his enlistment. By the summer of 1942 he was in uniform as a captain of Army Air Corps Intelligence, a position for which his knowledge of languages and happiness in travel were excellent qualifications. Quite apart from his satisfaction in fulfilling a moral duty, he believed that the enlistment would prove helpful to him as a literary artist.

> One of the dangers of the American artist [he has since observed] is that he finds himself almost exclusively thrown in with persons more or less in the arts. . . . So one of the benefits of military service, *one* of them, is being thrown into daily contact with non-artists, something a young American writer should consciously seek—his acquaintance should include those who have read only *Treasure Island* and have forgotten that.[20]

[20] Goldstone, p. 103.

Before reporting to the Air Corps Wilder completed *The Skin of Our Teeth* and put it into the hands of a producer, confiding to his sister Isabel the task of representing his interests while the play was readied for Broadway. Though somewhat difficult and demanding, it was recognized at once as a major work and ran profitably through the season. The run was, however, marked by a serious annoyance when, two months after the opening, the *Saturday Review of Literature* printed the exaggerated charge that in preparing the play, Wilder had plagiarized from *Finnegans Wake*. That he had made considerable use of Joyce's novel is beyond question, but it was naive, at the very least, of Wilder's accusers to assert that he had made a deliberate theft, since such a charge carries with it the suggestion that he had expected his source to go undetected forever. For the second time in his career his work gave rise to acrimonious controversy, and again he maintained a tactful silence. This uproar threatened far greater harm than the explosion of 1930, since it involved not only his scope as an artist, but his moral integrity. A restoration of calm occurred in the spring, when the play brought Wilder his third Pulitzer Prize. But by that time the Air Corps had dispatched him overseas, first to North Africa and then on to Italy, where he remained for the duration of the European war.

With the Bronze Star, the Legion of Merit, and a promotion to lieutenant colonel as the evidence of his wartime diligence, Wilder returned to civilian life in September 1945. The spirit of delighted inquiry remained with him as over the next three years he traveled between Europe and America to oversee productions of *Our Town* and *The Skin of Our Teeth* in England, France, and Germany, and acted the leading part of Mr. Antrobus in the latter play on Cape Cod in September 1946. The passing of his first half century was in no way the occasion for a lighter schedule of activity. The second half century began most auspiciously with fresh distinctions: honorary officership in the Order of the British Empire, conferred by Great Britain in December 1946, and an honorary doctorate awarded by Yale in June 1947. Yet time-consuming as the travels and non-literary obligations of these busy postwar years may have been, Wilder kept a good pace with his writing. In celebration of the centenary of the Century Association of New York, of which he was a member, he published a short dramatic burlesque, *Our Century*, late in 1947. This play, distributed only to the membership of the club, did not reach a large public and was not reviewed. In only two months, however, it was followed by a long-awaited major work: *The Ides of March*, his fifth novel.

Though doubtless disappointing to his Broadway following, Wilder's return to fiction with this lean, intricately constructed novel of the last months of Julius Caesar's life neither dismayed nor astonished his closest critics. Since the first production of *Our Town*, it had appeared that Wilder was in continual pursuit of new forms, and a glance back to the earlier works, in which he had turned from closet drama to meditative fiction to the sceneryless one-act play, confirmed the impression. Yet, setting its values as a work of art to one side for a moment, *The Ides of March* offers some surprises as a document revealing the writer's growth. Less to be expected than the shift in form is the influence upon the novel of the philosophy of Jean-Paul Sartre. During Sartre's postwar lecture tour of American universities, Wilder had made his acquaintance and had been stirred by his commentary on existentialism.[21] The atheistic implications of Sartre's philosophy were repugnant to Wilder, but the commitment to life, the demand upon the human spirit to proceed

[21] Isabel Wilder.

directly upon the path indicated by circumstances, was in accord with his own pattern of thought and action. Modified by Wilder's wish to affirm the presence of God amid conflicts seemingly beyond divine intervention, this aspect of existentialism is clearly discernible in the novel. It cannot, however, have been merely a matter of course for Wilder to fuse Christian and existentialist attitudes in the development of his narrative, for the tenets of Calvinism were too deeply imbedded in his personality to suffer even partial displacement without a struggle.

For the next seven years Wilder busied himself almost continuously with lecturing, the writing of essays, and travel, but produced no new play or novel. The suspicion arises that beneath the myriad enterprises lay an unconscious wish to put off the more difficult labors of literary invention. On the other hand, his eminence as a public figure was sufficient cause for a flood of invitations to speak, to teach, simply to be present, and, enjoying himself most when the tempo was highest, Wilder could not refuse. His new activities carried him back to the familiar literatures of France, Germany, and Spain, and led him at last to study and comment on the one great body of national writing which previously he had neglected: American literature. As a personal favor to Sartre, who wished to find an audience in America for his plays, he translated *Morts sans sépulture*, a melodrama of the French resistance; titled *The Victors*, the play was produced in Greenwich Village late in 1948 by the New Stages company, an impressive young off-Broadway group. Wilder was given credit as translator, but was not present at rehearsals and has never been able to ascertain whether the acted version was faithful to his translation.[22] By the time the production opened, he had left for Europe to give a few lectures at the center established by the Univer-

[22] Isabel Wilder.

sity of Chicago in Frankfurt-am-Main. On this trip abroad he also visited Berlin, then under Russian blockade and accessible only by means of the airlift. During the winter he gave thought to settling in Ireland for a while, but abandoned the notion in favor of his usual life on the move.

Returning home, he stayed in Hamden only briefly before journeying once more. The peripatetic life was his by choice, to be sure, but his travels on most occasions continued to have purposes beyond the sheer love of movement. Known everywhere as one of the most articulate and conversational American writers of his generation, he came to be much in demand as a lecturer in intellectual communities. He spoke in the summer of 1949 at the festival held in Aspen, Colorado, to commemorate the two hundredth anniversary of the birth of Goethe. In the academic year 1950–1951 he held the Charles Eliot Norton Professorship of Poetry at Harvard, a position generally considered to be the most honorific of endowed visiting professorships in letters. As the subject of the lectures which he delivered through the year, he chose "The American Characteristic in Classic American Literature"; to date, three of the lectures have been published. In the tradition of the professorial life, he delivered a paper at the 1950 meeting of the Modern Language Association of America, and this, consisting of conjectures on the dates of the early plays of Lope de Vega, he later published—also in the tradition of the professorial life. In still other ways the year was memorable: he was made a member of the Légion d'Honneur in April and received honorary degrees from Harvard and Northwestern in June. Another honor came in 1952, when the American Academy of Arts and Letters awarded him its Gold Medal for Fiction. When in the same year the United Nations Educational, Scientific, and Cultural Organization (UNESCO) called a conference on the arts in Venice, Wilder traveled to the meeting as Chief of the American Delegation.

The publicity surrounding his innumerable enterprises kept Wilder's name alive through the early 1950's, but did not forestall a slacking off of interest in his creative talent as year followed year with nothing more tangible than announcements from Hamden and Broadway of projects and plans. At last, in 1954, occurred a righting of the situation when at the prompting of Ruth Gordon, Garson Kanin (the actress's husband), and the English stage director Tyrone Guthrie, Wilder returned to the theater with *The Matchmaker*, a slightly revised version of *The Merchant of Yonkers*. With a cast led by Miss Gordon, for whom Wilder had originally designed what was now the title part, the play opened at the Edinburgh Festival in the summer of 1954 under Guthrie's direction. An immediate hit, it was taken to London, where it played through the following summer. The New York engagement, beginning in December 1955, was equally successful, vindicating Wilder's confidence in the farce so calamitously misdirected by Reinhardt. Though less distinguished than his two Pulitzer prize-winning plays, *The Matchmaker* proved an intelligent, and occasionally moving, piece of stage material.

This success, for which the credit belonged as much to the director and star as to the playwright, led to a second Wilder-Guthrie collaboration: *A Life in the Sun*, an adaptation of the *Alcestis* of Euripides. Produced at the Edinburgh Festival of 1955, the tragedy opened amid general hopes that with his first new work in over seven years Wilder could bring back to the stage the power of imagination evident in his earlier dramas. But in the new treatment of the plot, the tension and poetry of Euripides' great play vanished, leaving a flat and somewhat puzzling text. The play quickly sank under condemnatory reviews. Consolation for the failure came in 1957, when a German translation staged as *Die Alkestiade* received respectful attention at its first performance at Zurich. An operatic version with music by Louise Talma, employing the same title, also was well received at its première at Frankfurt-am-Main in 1962. Neither the play nor the opera has yet been produced in the United States.

Wilder has passed the decade since 1955 with his customary enjoyment of the moment, too critical of his prose to publish much of it, and seemingly indifferent to the possibility of a lowered reputation should he publish little more in the future. If he has failed to bring forward a work of stature since *The Ides of March*, he has kept faith with his public through half a dozen pieces varying in length, kind, and quality. In addition to writing the essays and plays already mentioned, he has fashioned a libretto from his own *The Long Christmas Dinner* for music by Paul Hindemith and has written a number—the total still undivulged—of short plays. For the opening of the American-financed Congress Hall of West Berlin in 1957, he offered two one-acts: *The Wreck of the 5:25*, starring Lillian Gish, and *Berniece*, starring Ethel Waters; un-happily, both plays went poorly, and he has neither published nor revised them.[23] The opera played its well-received première performances in Mannheim, Germany, in December 1961. But of all the recent work, only three one-acts presented off Broadway by the Circle in the Square theater from January to November 1962 have received wide circulation and exposure.

Yet Wilder continues to write, to be honored, and, by the mere mention of a project for his future, to make news. The grandest of the projects was also the most

[23] Isabel Wilder.

characteristic. Late in 1961, shortly before the Circle in the Square opening, Wilder announced his intention of writing two cycles of seven one-act plays each, one cycle to encompass the seven stages of man, and the other, the seven deadly sins.[24] No subject could have appeared more happily suited to Wilder's talents than the first of these, for he had never failed to take as his subject man in the abstract, a creature of incalculable variety, yet the same in all centuries. As for the second, though perhaps less appropriate for treatment by so optimistic a writer, it also promised well, for it was to combine with the cycle on the stages of life to present a summation of the knowledge of man Wilder had accumulated in six decades of study and observation. Theodore Mann and Jose Quintero, to whose theater Wilder intended to entrust all fourteen plays, found a large public ready to support the first three: *Infancy*, *Childhood*, and *Someone from Assisi*, the last-named representing the sin of lust. Offered on a single bill, they were advertised as *Plays for Bleecker Street*, the title indicating the location of the theater.

In March 1962, two months after the opening, Wilder arrived at a plan to insure the quiet necessary for the completion of the task he had set himself. He announced his decision to leave the East and settle for two years in the Arizona desert, where, away from the distractions of "cultivated conversation" (his phrase), he could get down to his work. At first he told the press that he would look for a retreat in the southernmost part of the state, somewhere between Tucson and Nogales, "a place where I can hit the bars with equal ease in both towns." But, he added, "No matter where it is, it's going to be my ideal of get-away quarters, a little white frame house with a rickety front porch where I can laze away in a straight-

[24] Arthur Gelb, "Thornton Wilder, 63, Sums Up Life and Art in New Play Cycle," New York *Times*, Nov. 6, 1961, pp. 1, 74.

backed wooden chair." [25] Soon, however, he recognized the unwisdom of so specific an announcement, for any hint of his whereabouts was sure to bring on a horde of reporters and friends. Reconsidering, he elected to drive out and take a house in whatever community promised greatest seclusion. Only his sister Isabel was to know its name, and she was enjoined to guard the secret from all inquirers. After a few more weeks in Hamden and an evening (April 30, 1962) with the Kennedy Cabinet in Washington, on which he read selections from his works, he climbed into his gray Thunderbird convertible and headed west.

As of the present moment, Wilder has not shown the results of his labors in exile. Nor, for that matter, has he reported that he has anything ready to show. The plan has not failed, but it has not gone forward according to the original terms. Wilder remained conscientiously at work for close to sixteen months in Arizona despite temptations which might have been expected to shake him from his resolve. He chose to stay away from the American première of the operatic version of *The Long Christmas Dinner*, in March 1963 at the Juilliard School in New York, although his old friend Hindemith was on hand to conduct the first two performances. Later, discovering himself included in the first group to receive the Presidential Medal of Freedom, he elected not to come to Washington for the reception held in July for those honored with the new decoration. In August, however, he flew to New York for a few days of theatergoing with his sister—the first break in his strict program of isolation. In the meantime he had come to a decision of much greater consequence to the success of his period of withdrawal from society. After long effort on the two cycles of plays, he

[25] "Wilder to Relax in Desert 2 Years," New York *Times*, March 3, 1962, p. 13.

suddenly conceived a plot for a novel and, setting the plays aside, began to write it. It is this, not the finished cycles, that we may next expect from him. For the time being the subject remains his secret.

Finally, at the close of 1963 came the inevitable decision to leave the desert for good. That Wilder departed ahead of schedule is less remarkable than that he stayed twenty of his projected twenty-four months, for not since his Air Corps days had he so drastically limited his moves. Still unwilling to take up the old round of social engagements and public appearances, and eager to go on with the novel, he sailed for Naples in January 1964, hoping to find in Italy another comfortable retreat. "I don't mean to be abrupt," he told reporters on arriving, "but I need privacy for a while. When it's all over I'll come back and explain what I've been doing. . . . I want nothing to do with newspapermen. No interviews—nothing. At least not for a year or so." [26] Before the year was over, he came back to America with the manuscript and, still in hiding, resettled himself for work. However short, his stay abroad augured well for the book, for it was in Italy that he first discovered in himself that sense of history with which for over forty years he has enriched our literature.

[26] "Hideaway in Italy Chosen by Wilder," New York *Times*, January 18, 1964, p. 15.

II. Beginnings:
Undergraduate Plays and
a Novel

During his college and Lawrenceville years Wilder wrote and published frequently enough to render suspect his complaint, as of 1928, of "the inertia that barely permits me to write at all."[1] His bibliographer lists thirty-eight short pieces printed from 1915 through 1925,[2] and these were followed by *The Cabala* in 1926. Had he given over all his time to writing, these works would not be impressive in number alone, for the shortest of them are very short indeed, and the novel owes its size to liberal spacing. But in his first adult decade he had relatively few hours of the week at his disposal; in view of the results, it is more likely than not that he found in literary composition a stimulus for getting on with his regular academic

---

[1] Wilder, *The Angel That Troubled the Waters and Other Plays in One Act* (New York: Coward-McCann, 1928), p. xiii.

[2] J. M. Edelstein, *A Bibliographical Checklist of the Writings of Thornton Wilder* (New Haven: Yale University Library, 1959), pp. 39–42.

chores. Many of the publications are plays in which three characters perform for only three minutes.

For something like twelve years, off and on until he published a collection of them in 1928, Wilder amused himself by writing these tricky, pedantic sketches. If the collection titled *The Angel That Troubled the Waters and Other Plays* had not appeared, it would be permissible to ignore them and move on to his more substantial prose. But a few of the plays are worth recalling in any case, and in committing them to print a second time, after magazine publication, Wilder seems to have expected them to find grateful readers.

Two of the plays are valuable advance signs of the professional career soon to begin. Among the first to be conceived,[3] though not published until 1920, was *Proserpina and the Devil*, a sketch which foreshadows Wilder's later, lengthier plays in its presentation of simultaneous views of past and present. Here the scene is an outdoor puppet-booth in seventeenth-century Venice; the characters, two puppeteers and their manager. The theme is that the myths of Greece and Rome still exist, but have taken a new form: Christianity. The cast of puppets is a mixture of figures from the two mythologies; it includes Proserpina, Demeter, Hermes, Gabriel, Abraham, and Satan. In manipulating these characters, the puppeteers confuse matters further by twice making Proserpina run toward, not away from, the Devil, thus forcing a confrontation of the old religion with the new. Another, more pointed early sketch, *The Death of the Centaur: A Foot-Note to Ibsen*, presents Shelley, or his ghost, before the curtain at a performance of Ibsen's *The Master Builder* at a moment when he takes the opportunity to tell the audience that he is the true author of the play. Its substance, he says, is the content of a poem he was on the point of writing on

[3] Wilder, *loc. cit.*

the day he drowned. In an oblique way the little play suggests that Wilder very early in life developed the idea that the great themes of literature may be borrowed and reborrowed without discredit to the borrower—that, in fact, such a process is inevitable. Shelley expresses the idea in this passage:

> Well, it is not a strange idea, or a new one, that the stuff of which masterpieces are made often drifts about the world waiting to be clothed with words. It is a truth that Plato would have understood that the mere language, the words of a masterpiece, are the least of its offerings. Nay, in the world we have come into now, the languages of the planet have no value; but the impulse, the idea of "Comus" is a miracle, even in heaven. Let you remember this when you regret the work that has been lost through this war that has been laid upon your treasurable young men. The work they might have done is still with you, and will yet find its way into your lives and into your children's lives. (pp. 86-87)[4]

Whatever virtues the two plays possess, they do not encourage a reader to proceed much further with the early writings. The returns from a review of all of them would diminish fairly quickly. A number of the pieces are the barest beginnings of drama; many of them show a tendency on Wilder's part to experiment with form before he had troubled to think up an adequate plot. Others suffer from that neo-Romantic quaintness which in 1917 Max Beerbohm lampooned exquisitely in "*Savonarola*" *Brown*; it is a languorous diction which does not suit the great events and personages involved. Of the rest, only one deserves mention: *Fanny Otcott*, in which the lady of the title is an eighteenth-century actress, Irish-bred,

---

[4] Page references following quotations in the text are to the first appearances of the works in book form, unless otherwise indicated. For full bibliographical information, see the Appendix.

and now in retirement, who after a separation of many years meets her old lover and for a moment, losing her brogue, takes the tone of her great tragic roles to rebuke him for calling their love a sin. What is impressive is Wilder's view of the actor's mentality, which permits Fanny to assume the mask at will, relying upon the force of her borrowed personality to drive away her one-time lover with a finality that she could never achieve in her own accent.

The most ambitious of the undergraduate projects was *The Trumpet Shall Sound*, a four-act play published in the *Yale Literary Magazine* from October 1919 through January 1920. Taking as his theme God's infinite capacity for pardoning even the worst of sinners, Wilder developed it in allegory, his favorite mode of expression at this time. God in the play is Peter Magnus, an indulgent master of four servants whom he leaves in charge of his house in his absence. The house is a mansion in Washington Square, New York City; the year is 1879. While Magnus is away, the servants, led by a young woman named Flora, let out rooms in the mansion to a considerable variety of persons, each of whom has committed at least one of the seven deadly sins. Flora has initiated this extraordinary scheme in the hope that a young sailor named Carlo, whom she loves, will come along to claim one of the rooms. Eventually he does so, but he has no great love for Flora, and although he consents to marry her in a mystical ceremony which she herself performs, he cannot display interest in her. There is an appealing craziness about the girl as she begs for some demonstration of love and wrings from him, during the ceremony, promises of future attentiveness. Soon, and quite predictably, Peter Magnus returns to his home, at first in the night without revealing himself, and again on the following day with the police. He explains to the police that he wishes to question the servants and the new tenants in the hope of judging the seriousness of their crime in taking over the house. It is a curious experiment, as the police see it, but they agree to let him speak to each offender. With an utter lack of passion he tries each case, only to decide that each must be forgiven. He can help all the sinners but Flora, who is so distressed over the loss of her sailor-lover that she kills herself. Hers is the sin of despair.

Had this play lain forever in the pages of the Yale *Lit*, where only the most devoted Wilder fans might spy it out, it would probably have escaped criticism. But Richard Boleslavsky's production of 1926 at the American Repertory Theatre, undertaken at the suggestion of Edith J. R. Isaacs of *Theatre Arts Monthly*,[5] brought the play before the public. This was the first professional performance of any of Wilder's plays. Understandably enough, the play failed, for the allegory is too obvious for comfort, and the action, except for the moments of Flora's frenzy over Carlo, is dull. What little else of merit may be claimed for the play consists in the delineation of the characters of these two lovers and in the psychological truth of the tension between them. Her overestimation of the man, the result of her unfulfilled desire, is apparent on his first entrance and at once creates sympathy for her. His wish to avoid a commitment is too familiar—it is what we have come to expect of sailors in drama—but it is nicely sustained in his fitful interludes with her as he retreats in alarm from her demands upon him. Beyond this, among the merits of the play, is the introduction of highly serviceable colloquial speech. At least while writing this play, if not before and not immediately afterward, Wilder recognized that for words of endearment or protest no language is more moving than the language of everyday living, for the good reason that it

[5] Isabel Wilder.

returns us to the simple speech patterns of our childhood and strikes note after note in harmony with our memories of the distant past. This was valuable knowledge, and in the plays of his maturity it proved its worth.

But to linger over even the best of these undergraduate compositions would be to impute to them more merit than they possess. Intelligent though some of them are, they have one serious defect. With the exception of *The Trumpet Shall Sound* they are somewhat too brief to make an effect. Wilder seems to have forgotten how distressing it is to a reader to come to the end of a work almost as soon as he has dug into it. In *The Trumpet*, however, it is length that is a major cause of failure— such great length that the allegory cannot sustain it. Not until the year in Rome was behind him and he had settled down to write in earnest for royalties did Wilder create a work of the right, or nearly the right, length for the ideas and feelings it was intended to project.

The setting of *The Cabala*, which Wilder began while still at the American Academy, is Rome and the regions nearby. But the milieu is not, Wilder has frequently reminded his critics, the Rome which he came to know. It is the city of the Black Roman aristocracy, of the "Cabala," in his own term, to whom because he saw them only from a distance he attributed a special, mysterious intelligence.

To refuse to believe Wilder's denial of intimacy with this level of society would be to discredit the novel as a work of art, a thing made up by a man of wide-ranging imagination. Yet, if the Cabalists are fantasy figures, the young American narrator of the novel, who is known only by the nickname "Samuele," and his friend James Blair are not strictly the author's inventions; they are a carry-over into the book of Wilder's academic background. The two men are specimens of a particular type of young

American: the university-bred amateur of huge talent, well informed, easy-going, mannerly, gregarious, and vastly eager to investigate the centers of power in every culture. This aspect of the novel—its presentation of the attitudes and folkways of the *beau monde* through the filter of an alert Eastern graduate's consciousness—places it within a minor but glittering stream of American fiction, with much of Henry James and Edith Wharton, most of F. Scott Fitzgerald, and, to take a more recent example, Frederick Buechner's *A Long Day's Dying.* In choosing the first-person technique, Wilder risked the identification of himself with Samuele, and it is indeed reasonable to point to resemblances between the living man and his fictional creature. The self-portrait, if that is what Wilder intended, has its charms, but it is not altogether flattering.

From first to last this young man, the product of a Calvinist upbringing, is intolerably stubborn and aloof. The habitual detachment revealed in his comments prompts mild laughter through most sections of the book and throws it into the mold of comedy, even though the world he describes is composed of the materials which usually go into the making of tragedy. The comic, cocky, ironic note is struck in the opening scene, as a train from the South speeds toward Rome. Wilder's deliberate scanting of serious matters begins on the first page, in a passage which permanently sets Samuele's personality:

> The train was overcrowded, because some tourists had discovered on the previous day that the beggars of Naples smelt of carbolic acid. They concluded at once that the authorities had struck a case or two of Indian cholera and were disinfecting the underworld by a system of enforced baths. The air of Naples generates legend. In the sudden exodus tickets for Rome became all but improcurable, and First Class tourists rode Third, and interesting people rode First. (pp. 7–8)

This describes the visitor's Italy; it barely hints at the

feeling of the real country. It is a clue to what follows in the novel, in which the views offered are the impressions of a tourist, not of a seasoned resident. Reflected in remarks which show no trace of sympathy, the comic separation of the visitor from his new environment blocks the reader from an impression of Italy as it is to the multitudes who will stay in it forever. The "enforced baths" and the air which "generates legend" are oblique indications of the speaker's view of life. They establish the tone of comedy of manners, and we see that we must adjust to that tone before we can locate the novel's theme. As for the passengers in First and Third, we get nothing definite to explain which class includes the narrator and James Blair; such a clue would be too personal a revelation from a man so reserved as Samuele.

To extend the narrator's emotional distance from the scene, Wilder makes him a newcomer to the Eternal City. For all his worldliness and his experience as an observer of mankind, he has not been much of a traveler, except in fantasy. "I would know my way about," he later remarks, "for my mind is built upon a map of the city that throughout the eight years of school and college had hung above my desk, a city so longed for that it seemed as though in the depth of my heart I had never truly believed I should see it" (p. 16). He knows it academically, as he knows most things, not by experience. Up to the closing pages of the novel the year's events seem to be a joke fate plays on him rather than deeply, personally meaningful activities, and he sees very little of the city other than its most remote, guarded, atypical part.

It is Blair, the traveling companion, who describes the Cabala to the narrator:

> They're very rich and influential. Everyone's afraid of them. Everyone suspects them of plots to overturn things.

Political?

No, not exactly. Sometimes.

Social swells?

Yes, of course. But more than that, too. Fierce intellectual snobs they are. . . . (p. 11)

In a moment he will add: "Each one of them has some prodigious gift, and together they're miles above the next social stratum below them. They're so wonderful that they're lonely. I quote. They sit off there in Tivoli getting what comfort they can out of each other's excellence."

In giving shape to these unusual beings, Wilder is inclined both to amuse and to preach to the reader. Although the speed and terseness of his prose hint that his feeling for the Cabalists is slight, he does not patronize them. The tone of the novel is an expression of awe in the presence of persons who despite their conservatism are vastly learned and vastly intelligent. They have read and assimilated everything; they seem, like Wilder himself, to have an almost perfect knowledge of music, which comes into the book on nearly every page. In the proletarian 1930's the attribution of such distinguished amateurism to the rich and powerful would be dismissed as the most egregious snobbery, and a quarter of a century later it is still likely to arouse suspicion in many intellectuals. Yet is is a hard fact that such persons as Wilder describes in *The Cabala* generally do possess the knowledge with which he credits them; it is this combination of wisdom and curiosity along with wealth which defines their class. Wilder works to elicit from the reader a sense of regret that they cannot find more satisfying ways of using what they have. In this aspect of the novel, at least, is a theme which transcends class interests.

Wilder is careful to point to the limitations of not only the Cabalists but of Samuele as well. Ostensibly this young American has come to Rome to study ancient history, but as the year goes by he loses interest in formal study. There are too many adventures for that: the adventures of furnishing a new apartment, of meeting new people, even of comforting a dying poet. Not until we watch him finishing all these affairs do we see that he has obtained valuable insights into the minds of the Cabalists. It is as though Wilder were at pains to justify the confidence which Samuele wins from them by demonstrating certain similarities of his outlook to theirs. The mocking tone never ceases as his interests reveal themselves. Like the Cabalists he is quite satisfied with his own taste and happy in his general knowledge of the arts. These qualities give an aristocratic cast to his bearing, although it is true that he does not possess the means to indulge his tastes to the full. Thus, on the decoration of his rooms:

> During the first week Blair helped me find and fit out an apartment. It consisted of five rooms in an old palace across the river and within stone's-throw of Santa Maria in Trastevere. The rooms were high and damp and bad Eighteenth Century. . . . We passed two days in choosing chairs and tables, in loading them upon carts and personally conducting them to our mean street; in haggling over great lengths of gray-blue brocade before a dozen shops, always with a view toward variety in stains and unravellings and creases; in selecting from among the brisk imitations of ancient candelabra those which most successfully simulated age and pure line. (pp. 16–17)

Samuele, like many young men of his class, is too poor to be utterly fastidious in matters of decoration, but obviously he has the knack of making do. Only a few years earlier F. Scott Fitzgerald's Amory Blaine was exhibiting all the signs of misery on New York's Upper West Side, without the consolation of candelabra in pure line. But Amory was in love, and we have no reason to suspect that Samuele is capable of that emotion; the possessor of a fine eye for brocade rarely is. It is his willingness to settle for *things* rather than persons in his emotional life that gives Samuele the ability to interest himself in the innermost circle of Roman society, where fascination with things runs high. He is, of course, subject to the Cabalists' scrutiny in turn. Although they do not have an opportunity to watch him decorate his flat, they have the satisfaction of discovering, through close interrogation, that he and Blair are of "good family."

Nowhere else is the question of how much Wilder has drawn upon his own personality so pressing as in this parade of the evidence of taste and learning. Samuele makes it sufficiently clear as he describes the Cabalists that he is as familiar as they with all varieties of serious music, with the writings of the Church Fathers, and with a mass of miscellaneous tracts, including Freud's monograph on Leonardo. But a trace of self-mockery is always present in this side of Samuele's character. "One no longer cared to hear *Salome*, but *Petrushka* was being danced after it, at ten-thirty," he observes (p. 127), and the words drip with the snobbery of the man whose social education has occurred at the expense of his humanity. But the comment reveals such extraordinary elegance that its final effect is of pure burlesque, as though the boy of narrow religious background were bursting to show how far along in the world he had come. Here, and in all such passages, a conviction arises beyond the words that in Wilder's own opinion knowledge divorced from humanity is a tolerably amusing evil, but an evil nevertheless. One coolly written scene, the last of the opening section of the novel, fixes the impression.

In this scene Blair takes Samuele, on their first evening in Rome, immediately following their initial meeting with the Cabala, to call on a young English poet who is dying of consumption in a small apartment near the

Spanish Steps. The identity of the poet is clear at once:
he is John Keats, who died in just such quarters a century
before Wilder's year in Rome. At first Samuele blunders
amazingly in conversation with him:

> By the way, are there any books you'd like us to lend
> you?
> Thank you. That would be fine.
> What, for instance?
> Anything.
> Think of one you'd like especially.
> Oh, anything. I'm not particular. Only I suppose
> it would be hard to find any translations from the Greek?
> Here I offered to bring in a Homer in the original and
> stammer out an improvised translation.
> Oh, I should like that most of all, he cried. I know
> Chapman's well.
> I replied, unthinking, that Chapman's was scarcely
> Homer at all, and suddenly beheld a look of pain, as of
> a mortal wound, appear upon his face. To regain control
> of himself he bit his finger and tried to smile. I hastened
> to add that in its way it was very beautiful, but I could
> not recall my cruelty; his heart seemed to have com-
> menced bleeding within him. (p. 46)

Such a moment of social blundering is rare in Samuele's
career. Ordinarily he is more than able to muster the
phrases required by the occasion. Here, however, as
though to establish not merely his fallibility but the
general absurdity of learning separated from human
understanding, he drops a comment which belittles the
dying man's intelligence. But in continuing the conversation he finds a way to atone partially for the offense:

> His face showed clearly what matter pleased him; I
> experimented on it, and discovered that he was hungry
> for hearing things praised. He was beyond feeling
> indignant at abuses, beyond humor, beyond sentiment,
> beyond interest in any bits of antiquarian lore. Appar-

ently for weeks together in the wretched atmosphere of
the sick-room Francis his companion had neglected to
speak highly of anything and the poet wanted before he
left the strange world to hear some portion of it praised.
... Most of all he desired the praise of poetry. (pp. 47–48)

What follows is a list of the great poets—a list in which the
dying man insists that his name belongs.

The idea of the efficacy of praise, and of praise of
praise, for abating the shock of death is somewhat
difficult to grasp on first encounter. Wilder has since
demonstrated its importance to him by using it a second
and third time. In *The Woman of Andros* a dying woman is
herself the person to praise "the world and all living"
and to accept from the gods "all things, the bright and
the dark" (p. 107). Julius Caesar in *The Ides of March*
comforts the dying Catullus precisely as Samuele comforts Keats, and in the same city. The principle embodied
in the act requires for acceptance a disposition not only
to love life in its infinitely various aspects, but to enjoy
each event as it occurs with such intensity as to recognize
perfectly, before death comes, how much pleasure one has
experienced through one's years. From this it should
follow that in a deeply felt life the event of death itself will
bring on a state of confident expectation, though Wilder
never carries the idea so far. Samuele only half under-
stands his own words; for him such talk is an almost
desperate measure in the poet's small rooms, a gesture
undertaken for want of a better. But his speech adds to the
meaning of the novel, for it throws into relief the Cabalists'
frenzied efforts to reach certain unattainable goals and
reveals their undertakings to be the neurotic drives of
persons for whom the ordinarily pleasant and useful
activities of "the good life" are not enough.

Each of the three central sections, which as a group
follow Samuele's interview with the poet, presents a

Cabalist seized by a relentless passion, the effect of which is so fierce that it reduces its victim to futility and leads to actions which are gross parodies of human behavior. In each instance the narrator responds to a plea for help. It is his task to save the Cabalists, either by guiding them toward normality or by rearranging the world in such a way as to make the Cabalists' behavior the norm. Each of these distracted persons is older than the last; the first is a boy of sixteen, the second a woman in her thirties, and the third a quite elderly lady. Samuele answers each appeal, only to find that his inherent Puritanism has rendered him too insensitive to serve as nurse or mentor to persons raised in another tradition. He, despite his willingness to praise life, is no less narrow than the Cabalists. He is an eternal joke, but of a particularly cruel kind: a dilettante of the emotions whose ministrations lead to disaster. These Romans are too complex to be understood by a native of the New World.

Marcantonio, the youngest son of an impoverished and seemingly ancient lady of quality, is Samuele's first case. The boy is afflicted with such deep-seated hatred of women that he delights in degrading them sexually. On first appearance he impresses everyone as a normal young man with a young man's taste for fast cars and athletics. But this we understand to be only the surface of his character, for his mother, Her Highness Leda Matilda Colonna duchessa d'Aquilanera, has already told the narrator of her great anxiety over his sexual excesses. "Now listen," she says to the American on their first meeting, "I have a son of sixteen. He is important because he is somebody. How you say?—he is a personage" (p. 59). But he is also a constant visitor of brothels. Because Elizabeth Grier, an American member of the Cabala, has led her to believe that all young Americans are *vieilles filles*, she has conceived the notion that Samuele is precisely the person to impress upon Marcantonio the enormity of his sins; it would seem to be her thought that such a man as Samuele would find them particularly abhorrent. Although Samuele responds somewhat diffidently to her suggestion, he is enough amused by it to spend a weekend in Marcantonio's company, but without first promising to take the boy to task.

To convince the narrator of the seriousness of the situation, Donna Leda asks Cardinal Vaini, the favorite prelate of the Cabalists, also to be on hand. This Prince of the Church, one of the strongest characters in the novel, plays a part in all three episodes and serves as a focal point for the Cabalists' attitudes toward religion. Old, subtle, wise, he is tolerant of the excesses of his friends and hopeful that they will ultimately gain self-knowledge, yet unwilling to point directly to the course of action leading to it. To the American Puritan, however, his attitudes are utterly strange, perhaps exotic. Samuele cannot understand the principle whereby the Cardinal proposes that he work with Marcantonio only to the extent of rendering the young man acceptable to eligible girls, without demanding a fundamental change in his personality.

The narrator does bring about that change, but not with happy results. When at last Marcantonio pours out the anguish which for months he has stored away even from his confessor, Samuele deals with him in a manner which anyone less innocent than he himself would describe as brutal. "Heaven only knows what New England divines lent me their remorseless counsels," he remarks (p. 98). He forces the boy to see that he has fallen so deeply into lust that his mind is disintegrating. He delivers, or so he reports, a Puritannical tirade. The boy is shocked by Samuele's severity and in violent reaction makes a sexual conquest of his own half-sister. Then, overcome by shame, abandoned by Samuele, whose only thought is for his own "poor sick head . . . so full of the erotic narratives of the week" (p. 103), Marcantonio kills himself. The blame for the tragedy rests with two persons: Samuele, because of the stupidity of his conduct, and Donna Leda, because of her essentially self-centered drive to make a respectable match for her son. The mother has given a moment or two of thought to the boy's welfare, it is true, but her primary motive in engaging Samuele was the protection of her own status as the head of a venerable family.

The second episode introduces the charming French-woman, Alix d'Espoli, the wife of an Italian prince. In describing her, Wilder suggests that she is the full flower of the aristocracy as it came to be in the seventeenth century. She is gracefully learned and intuitively ingratiating, the possessor of a splendid gift for languages, unfailing wit, and the knack of falling into the mood of her companion of the moment. But clouded faith and psychic malfunctions combine to trouble her, as with each of the others whom Samuele tries to assist. Unhappy with her Italian husband, she continually falls in love with Nordic men, who represent a type as different as possible from the prince. These, however, are not the men who can return her love; they are cool and impersonal, whereas she is warm and greedy for emotional experience. It is her misfortune to meet and fall in love with James Blair, who is one of the unresponding sort. His indifference to her, no less than her emotionalism, finds its explanation in Freudian psychology: "What kind of a stupid mother could he have had?" Alix exclaims (p. 117). Unprepared for such aloofness, she contemplates suicide on the night when he flees Rome to avoid her suffocating affection.

In the final pages of her chapter Wilder presents Alix's spiritual progress. Upon recovering her will to live, she embarks frenetically on a series of social engagements in the hope of putting Blair out of her thoughts. Ultimately she attends a séance in the rooms of a Rosicrucian seer, whose gatherings have included all Rome. This is her nadir; her very presence in the seer's apartment supplies the evidence that she has become confused in her religious beliefs. Her punishment is appropriately severe: at the séance she catches a glimpse of Blair, who is in Rome on an unannounced visit. After this comes a period of soul-searching, represented by a renewed interest in the arts, and then follows a period of penitence, represented by volunteer work in hospitals. When she has completed these steps toward grace, she returns to the Cabala, her old self again, and receives a prodigal's welcome from Father Vaini. Yet at the end of the chapter she faints on hearing Blair's name, and the dangers of monomania are underscored.

The third episode presents a farther remove of the Cabala from the familiar concerns of the world. In this chapter, it is an old woman, Mlle Astrée-Luce de Mor-fontaine, who comes to Samuele with a problem. Not only is she old, she is distant, a second-century Christian, so simple in her piety that any mention of such primitive symbols of Christianity as the fish and the pelican will put her into a daze. Her request is by far the most remarkable made to the narrator—so remarkable that it tends to confirm his suspicion that she is mad. She wishes him to appeal to the Cardinal to write an argument for the incorporation of the Divine Right of Kings into Church dogma, for she believes that only by this measure can the future of European civilization be secured. Once more the death knell of Europe sounds in the novel; we have heard it before in the grim fate of Marcantonio and reports of the growing strength of Fascism.

By now the failure of the Cabalists' schemes is to be expected. In view of what has already occurred in the novel, it is no surprise that the Cardinal declines the task. His idea of religion is highly personal—too personal for the Church—and it does not include such fripperies as plague the mind of the old woman. Religion has filled out the lives of both of them, but in quite different ways. To Astrée-Luce it is the authority of the Church, which the pressures of the modern world now threaten. For the Cardinal, it is not an authoritarian force, but the direct, simple consolation of the people, and as such does not require the elaborate machinery of the Vatican.

Astrée-Luce fails in her effort to promulgate faith from above, through the Church, and the Cardinal is no longer strong enough to cultivate it directly and swiftly in the people, as in the dim past he succeeded in doing among the Chinese. Samuele speaks to the Cardinal on behalf of the old woman, but his effort falls short of its goal. Astrée-Luce suffers a temporary weakening of her faith when the Cardinal belligerently questions her acceptance of fundamental tenets of the Church. Later, in the presence of the other Cabalists, she accuses him of being the devil incarnate; she then draws a pistol from an arrangement of flowers and tries to shoot him. The scene, despite its serious moral point, is the most wildly comic of the novel; nothing could be more unexpected than that this pious, aged daughter of the Church should try to kill one of its most eminent spokesmen. She misses, and the bullet lodges in the ceiling, cracking it and cracking the façade of the Cabala as well. Equally futile is the Cardinal's desire to return to the people. He sails for China, but en route falls into a fatal illness.

The novel ends with a brief epilogue whose purpose is to demonstrate the moral significance of all this experience. Before his departure for America, Samuele talks with Elizabeth Grier about the extraordinary society in which he has spent his year. It is obvious to both that the Cabala cannot last. Although the members may be reincarnations of the Olympian gods, as Miss Grier believes, they have now lost their great strength. We have observed their gradual decline through the central episodes, each of which has been a chapter in failure: failure, with Marcantonio, of the gods to reproduce themselves; with Alix, to attract new worshippers; with Astrée-Luce and the Cardinal, to broaden their powers. On the last night of his voyage home, Samuele discovers, with the aid of Virgil, whom he conjures, that he must help to build a new city in the New World, for Rome, along with all that it has represented, is certain to fade. For centuries it has stood as the citadel of the aristocracy, that ancient guiding force of Europe. But now it matters little, for the aristocracy itself will soon vanish. It has vitiated itself through sheer self-absorption, as revealed in the Cabalists' preoccupation with futile or foolish affairs and inadequate comprehension of the serious issues of twentieth-century life. From this it should follow that Samuele must learn from their mistakes, the mistakes of history, by breaking out of the confines of his own limited interests. He must, in short, learn the meaning of his own remarks to the dying Keats.

The value of this theme is obscured somewhat by the portentous language of the epilogue and the difficulty of estimating the personality of the narrator. The remarks on the Olympian deities and the appearance of Virgil detract, unfortunately, from the pleasures of reading of the aristocracy in an agreeably mocking tone; with these late intrusions the language of the novel soars to a height too great for its subject. But the weakness in the delineation of Samuele is the more serious of the novel's two defects. Too late for comfort comes the awareness that we have been witnessing the last phase of his education, so satisfied is he with his new environment throughout all but the last pages. For this reason the book may easily be mistaken for a gaudy fantasy of patrician life when in fact it is a highly didactic novel developed in comic terms. Wilder was not to return to comic fiction for another decade, and then with a marked difference in technique. In the remainder of the 1920's his moral sense was to deepen and to find candid, as opposed to ironic, expression in the treatment of plot and character.

III. Voyages into History

ON ITS PUBLICATION in 1926 *The Cabala* mildly stimulated the curiosity of the critical press, but did not receive high praise. Over the years, as Wilder's reputation rises with each new work, the Roman story is brought out of the vast limbo where most first novels rest, is compared unfavorably with the new novel or play, is searched for biographical details, and then is dropped until the next work comes into print. The history of *The Bridge of San Luis Rey*, on the other hand, has included two Hollywood productions, a television adaptation, and continuous availability in a variety of hardcover and softbound printings, in addition to the Pulitzer Prize. From the outset, it has been a popular favorite.

Turning away from the modern world for the time being, Wilder set his new novel in eighteenth-century Peru. The setting is so distant from the areas explored by most of the established writers of the 1920's that Wilder's reasons for choosing it have frequently come under question. This was, after all, the decade when Willa Cather's tough-minded novels of the prairies and the Southwest were achieving the status of minor classics as soon as published, when Sinclair Lewis, for all his roughness of style, reached the best-seller lists with each novel of the Midwest, and when even the expatriates Ernest Hemingway and Gertrude Stein wrote with a patently deep attachment to their homeland. In attempting to account for Wilder's neglect of America in his fiction, Malcolm Cowley has suggested that, unlike his famous contemporaries, he has never lived long enough in any one region to put down roots in American soil.[1] He had spent his formative years not in one or (like Willa Cather) two places, but in Wisconsin, California, China, and California again, and having so many homes, he had none so distinctly his that it could serve as a base upon which to erect a fictional image of his country. Not even the act of building his own house in Hamden was a guarantee that he would rest in one place for long; when the spirit prompted, he was off again—not, it is true, to take up residence abroad like Gertrude Stein, Hemingway, or Fitzgerald, but simply to move about. Ultimately the three cross-country lecture tours that he made after 1929 and the six half-years that he spent at the University of Chicago gave him a certain familiarity with the Midwest that he was to put to use in a fourth novel, and at least by 1938 he had observed New England closely enough to sketch it faintly in *Our Town*. But it is doubtful that in the 1920's he was equipped to compete with the American regionalists, even had he cared to try.

Of nearly equal consequence in the making of *The Bridge* was the range and continuity of Wilder's learning. As both an instinctive and academic scholar, he was inevitably persuaded by his researches to give them shape in his fiction. His recent study in Romance languages at Princeton makes itself apparent in *The Bridge*, through

[1] Malcolm Cowley, introduction, *A Thornton Wilder Trio* (New York: Criterion Books, 1956), p. 4.

allusions to Spanish literature of the Golden Age, through his fashioning of one character, the Marquesa de Monte-mayor, upon the personality and literary pursuits of Mme. de Sévigné, and through the borrowing of another, Camila Perichole, from Prosper Mérimée's *La Carosse du Saint Sacré*, which also provides the setting. The desire is always present in the scholar to make extensive use of his learning. With Wilder it manifested itself in fiction and drama, not, as with most academic men, in bio-graphical, philological, or critical essays, though the initial impulse is the same for all. Considering this root quality in the scholarly personality, it is reasonable to say that the civilizations which Wilder had studied were as vivid to him as the life of his own time and place. That he had not traveled to Peru was of no consequence to him. Three decades later he remarked to an interviewer from the *Paris Review* that "the journey of the imagination to a remote place is child's play compared to a journey into another time. I've often been in New York, but it's just as preposterous to write about the New York of 1812 as to write about the Incas." [2]

Another influence, apparent in *The Cabala* also, was the humanistic criticism of More and Babbitt. It manifests itself in two aspects of Wilder's art: the absence of violence and squalor and the acceptance of Christian values. In the first and second episodes of *The Cabala* Wilder describes the exotic coloration given to life by troubled belief; although he is sometimes scornful of or impatient with the wrong-headed characters of that novel, his tone is for the most part only mildly ironic. He treats this subject again in *The Bridge*, but in a quite different mode. We should note that the setting is a place where the

[2] Richard H. Goldstone, "Thornton Wilder," in *Writers at Work: The Paris Review Interviews*, ed. Malcolm Cowley (New York: Viking Press, 1958), pp. 104–105.

relationship of God to man made itself felt in all the details of life, as it does not in twentieth-century America.

Structurally as well as thematically, *The Bridge of San Luis Rey* resembles *The Cabala*. Wilder again employs a sketchy framing story to bring unity to three tales which are only partially related in content. There are, however, certain differences in the use of this device in the second novel, but not such as work to Wilder's advantage. In the frame of *The Bridge*, the function of Samuele goes to a young, earnest Franciscan friar, Brother Juniper, who resembles Samuele in his presumptuousness, but does not narrate the events and does not take part in them. His presence is little more than an excuse for the three episodes, and that little serves only to establish his own interpretation of them, which eventually Wilder overthrows in favor of a superior interpretation. When Brother Juniper, on a day in 1714, sees an old slat-and-vine bridge near Lima break and send five travelers to death in the gorge below, he begins a search through the history of their lives for pieces of evidence that God purposely let them die, for he is certain that the event is no accident. The five are an old man, a middle-aged woman, a young man, an adolescent girl, and a little boy. Unlike the characters of *The Cabala*, they have not all played important roles in one another's lives, and none has known the young man who now takes a surpassing interest in them. Compared to Samuele's old-maidish fussing over the Cabalists, which in itself contributes abundantly to the theme of the narrative, Brother Juniper's presence is an ungainly expository contrivance, and his by-the-book religiosity, weighing so much good in each victim of the fall against so much evil, is too obviously unavailing in the search for the meaning of the disaster.

"Yet for all his diligence," the omniscient author says, "Brother Juniper never knew the central passion of

Doña Maria's life; nor of Uncle Pio's, not even of Esteban's. And I, who claim to know so much more, isn't it possible that even I have missed the very spring within the spring?" (p. 23). Thus taking the reader into his confidence with the suggestion that any system for measuring the quality of a life is certain to fail, Wilder begins the three short episodes which lead the five travelers up to the fatal moment. He himself does not give a direct interpretation of the event, but leaves it to the reader to discover what common concerns of all five have caused them to walk simultaneously over the bridge to death. In the last pages of the novel the alert reader's findings are given voice by Madre Maria del Pilar, Abbess of the Convent of Santa Maria de las Rosas, the one character who has knowledge of the entire group of victims:

> "Even now," she thought, "almost no one remembers Esteban and Pepita, but myself. Camila alone remembers her Uncle Pio and her son; this woman, her mother. But soon we shall die and all memory of those five will have left the earth, and we ourselves shall be loved for a while and forgotten. But the love will have been enough; all those impulses of love return to the love that made them. Even memory is not necessary for love. There is a land of the living and a land of the dead and the bridge is love, the only survival, the only meaning." (pp. 234–5)

By this time the "spring within the spring" of each life has come to light, and for each it is the same: the desire for love. The episodes demonstrate that the fall of the bridge is actually a spring *into* love; on this point the deliberations of Brother Juniper, as well as the brief first-person comments of the author, are dust thrown into the reader's eyes, as though purposely to make difficult the analysis of a novel which is by no means complex.

The first of the central chapters probes the troubles of

a rich old woman nearly maddened by maternal love, and of a young girl caught up in the frenzy of the old woman's life. Doña Maria, Marquesa de Montemayor, possesses tremendous intellectual power and the looks and manners of a street-beggar. She spends the first three weeks of every month in an alcoholic fog and the last week in the furious process of gathering fact and lore about the viceregal court of Peru to send in beautifully composed letters to her daughter in Spain. Her life is utterly at the disposal of her daughter; ugly, slovenly, and unloved, she cares for nobody else in the world. Among the residents of Lima, not one is aware of the old woman's stylistic skill; nor, we are given to understand, is it until long after her death that the letters pass into the world's literature.

Doña Clara, the daughter, is worse than ungrateful for her mother's affection and the expensive gifts which betoken it. Beautiful, but unresponsive to attention except as it comes from the artists and writers whom she patronizes, she has deliberately chosen a Spaniard, not a Peruvian colonial, from among her suitors, so as to escape Peru and the presence of her mother. It is Doña Clara's husband, the Conde d'Abuirre, who preserves the brilliant letters, not the daughter herself. Yet not even the good-natured husband values them to the full; "he thought that when he had enjoyed the style he had extracted all their richness and intention, missing (as most readers do) the whole purport of literature, .which is the notation of the heart" (p. 34). With this hint it becomes impossible for us to miss the notation of the Marquesa's heart, which yearns incessantly for any sign of love from Doña Clara. Wilder implies that neither mother nor daughter is morally correct in her attitude; somewhere between their respective positions is the ground on which they should meet. Doña Clara is unnatural in her contempt for her mother, but Doña Maria is equally at fault for neglecting body and soul out of blind love. Not until the Marquesa becomes aware of her error can her life take a sensible direction. Once she begins to understand herself, she will receive a greater love than her daughter has the power to give.

As a kind of comment on the erratic ways of the Marquesa, Wilder provides the young Pepita, sent out from the convent by Madre Maria del Pilar to live with Doña Maria. For this girl the Abbess has a special regard; Pepita is her choice as successor to herself in directing the orphanage and hospital for incurables in Lima. Madre Maria is also in danger of letting her feeling become an obsession, but the danger is slight, since she is able to part with the girl for the sake of the Marquesa. Pepita returns the Abbess's affection more fully than the older woman seems to realize; to her the Abbess is the source of all good on earth. Because Madre Maria so directs her, she goes into the home of the Marquesa with complete willingness to serve, no matter how neglected or abused she may feel in the household. Mistress and servant have objects of love which neither can see clearly, although Pepita is far more rational in her love for the Abbess than Doña Maria in her love for Doña Clara.

One touching gesture from Pepita at last releases the Marquesa from the durance of her feeling for the icily elegant daughter. It occurs at the shrine of Santa Maria de Cluxumbuqua, some little distance from Lima. To that shrine the Marquesa goes, attended as always by Pepita, as soon as she receives the news, casually intro-duced into a letter about other matters, of Doña Clara's pregnancy. Her only thought is to pray for a safe delivery, but it is questionable whether the unborn child or the expectant mother is her primary concern. Religion has long since thinned out for her to prayer addressed to a

God with only one attribute: the power to instill affection in a daughter's heart. At the shrine she prays so long that she worries lest she anger God by importuning too insistently. Meanwhile Pepita, now very lonely in her company, has written hesitantly and secretly for a word of comfort from the Abbess:

> *Though I never see you I think of you all the time and I remember what you told me, my dear mother in God. I want to do only what you want, but if you could let me come back for a few days to the convent, but not if you do not wish it. But I am so much alone and not talking to anyone, and everything. Sometimes I do not know whether you have forgotten me and if you could find a minute to write me a little letter or something, I could keep it, but I know how busy you are. . . .* (p. 80)

Her loneliness, her mistress's lack of consideration, and the harassment she has suffered from the other servants have at last become too heavy to bear. A chance notice of this letter at Cluxumbuqua at once changes the Marquesa's life. She is at first amazed that the Abbess possesses the power to evoke so much affection from Pepita, then ashamed that she herself has not given thought to the girl's emotional needs, and ultimately more deeply ashamed, on hearing Pepita's decision not to post the letter because it is not "brave," of her own selfishness in continually demanding a demonstration of love from Doña Clara. In this new light her old ways become contemptible to her, and she aspires to the courage to begin at last to live. On the journey home, mistress and servant set foot on the fatal bridge.

From this examination of excessive maternal love Wilder turns to a description of a variety of neurotic affection rare in fiction: the feeling of one twin for his brother which is so intense that it approaches homosexual yearning. Wilder's comments on the young man's feelings are, however, by no means sensational. Esteban, whose life is devoted to his brother, is not aware of the implications of his passion; it is enough to say that he has unknotted "that secret from which one never quite recovers, that even in the most perfect love one person loves less profoundly than the other" (p. 100). In the expository passages of their chapter, Wilder gives the information that Manuel and Esteban were raised by the Abbess, who found them in a basket outside the convent door, worked as boys at odd jobs around the city's ecclesiastical buildings, and at the time of their appearance in the novel are writing letters for the city's illiterates. Life for each is intolerable when the other is absent, and although they occasionally have relations with women, they derive greater comfort from each other than from all other sources. But once they take employment with Camila Perichole, Lima's greatest actress, their intimacy dissolves. The result is tragedy.

Camila, the Viceroy's unfaithful mistress, has already made her appearance in the novel; in the first episode she visits the Marquesa to beg her forgiveness for burlesquing her one evening in the theater. In the second episode she unwittingly comes between the two brothers as the object of Manuel's adoration. When Esteban sees this new direction in his brother's life, he is precipitated into despair.

As the chapter pushes toward its conclusion, the agony of Esteban broadens into an all-consuming sorrow. Born centuries before the age of psychological jargon, and poorly educated even for his time and place, he cannot find the words for what he feels. But even the inarticulate can be eloquent when occasions press upon them heavily enough; in the phrase which Wilder gives to Esteban is a world of sensitivity: "I'm in your way" (p. 115.) When a neglected wound causes the death of Manuel, Esteban adopts his name and is mistaken by everyone for his brother. This is his only way of keeping the absent twin with him. He finds no new source of emotion; not even the Abbess, whom both brothers have always loved, can now enter his world. Yet, despite his grave sense of dislocation, he agrees to put to sea with one Captain Alvarado, an eternal ocean voyager who has been unable to find contentment anywhere since the death of his young daughter many years earlier. Thus begins the association of two men from whom the only reason for living has disappeared.

Esteban by now has suffered a partial loss of mind. Knowing that suicide is a sin, he would like to find some way of meeting death that is just short of self-slaughter, and accordingly he exacts from the captain a promise that he will be given the most dangerous chores on the voyage. Even with such an end in view he would not make the voyage at all were it not for one notion which the understanding captain steers him toward: the thought that with his earnings he will be able to buy a present for the Abbess. It is the only thought he has had for another person since his brother's death, and, faint though it is, it leads him to redemption. The journey to the sea takes the two men to the chasm near Cluxumbuqua, and while the captain goes down the hill with his merchandise, Esteban sets foot on the bridge.

At this point in the narrative Wilder's theme has already received very full expression. The story of Uncle Pio, which makes up the third section, is written at least as well as the others, but it is an unnecessary decoration upon the novel's structure. Like the other victims, the old man has given all his passion to one person, and with such fury that all else in life has meaning only insofar as it relates to her. His adored is Camila Perichole, whom he discovered when at the age of twelve she sang ballads in cafes for a living. Under his tutelage she was to become the outstanding performer of her generation: a better performer than she could ever know, since she has not had an opportunity to observe her only rivals, the actresses of Spain itself. Uncle Pio's enthusiasm for the dramatic literature of the seventeenth century has found its perfect voice in Camila, and since meeting her he has thought of nothing except the development of her skills.

Wilder moves quickly over the Perichole's training to concentrate on the period of her success and the years which follow it. Having left the stage at thirty, she settles into a mountain villa near Cluxumbuqua, takes on airs of grandeur, and surrounds herself with fashionable people. To remove all traces of the past, she casts off Uncle Pio and advises him not to appear in her presence. Wilder hints that the new life gives her a certain satisfaction, but hints further, by mentioning her great temper, that it is limited, as is the satisfaction of anyone who cannot make his self-image become a fact without violently distorting his personality. But even the small pleasure of conducting a salon fades when she suffers a virulent attack of smallpox. Afraid to show her face, she isolates herself permanently in the mountains with only her epileptic son for a companion. Again Uncle Pio steps in, and again she rebuffs him. He is the least amorous of Pygmalions; the love he gives, like the love of each of the group of victims, is never consciously erotic. Nevertheless, he cannot bear to be away from her. Ultimately he promises to leave her forever if she will grant him permission to take the little boy, Don Jaime, to Lima for one year, where he can receive an education. Obviously, he has the thought of keeping a tie with Camila by performing a service for her son which is beyond her powers. Yet it is clear that he too has at last shown regard for another person than the one he thus far allowed to shape his life. As soon as Camila consents to the scheme, he and the boy depart for Cluxumbuqua. The bridge lies in their route.

In review, the victims of the bridge are these: an old woman whose daughter spurns her affection, an adolescent girl who lives only for the affection of an older woman, a young man whose sole object of love is dead, an old man whose sole object of love has rejected him, and a child whose mother is too self-involved to give him the affection he requires. For one reason or another, each stands apart from human society: two because they are old and unkempt; two because they are orphans; and the fifth because he is chronically ill. And with the exception of Don Jaime, each has added to the barrier between himself and society by failing to respond to any activity which does not involve his beloved. Pepita is at only slightly greater odds with the rest of humanity than Don Jaime, but even she must think constantly of the one person she loves in order to sustain herself, and it is not until she begins to recognize the selfishness inherent in her distress in the Marquesa's household that she is allowed to escape through death. Perhaps it is a flaw in the novel that Don Jaime's life so poorly fits the pattern set by the other characters; yet he resembles them in part by agreeing to leave his mother, the only person whom he adores, and to go down to Lima with Uncle Pio. But, for that matter, Wilder flatly asserts that it is difficult, if not impossible, to find patterns in existence, and Brother Juniper is burned as a heretic for trying to do so.

Although *The Bridge of San Luis Rey* is imperfect, its faults are not ruinous. Whatever they may be, they are not caused by such deficiencies in taste and wisdom as are evident in most American religious fiction—the novels of Lloyd C. Douglas provide suitable examples for comparison. *The Bridge* is not sentimental; it offers no promises of earthly rewards and no overestimation of the worth of the characters. Nor does it speak out against active participation in this life in favor of patient waiting for the life to come. Yet, noting that many persons have misunderstood his intention, Wilder has himself remarked: "Only one reader in a thousand notices that I have asserted a denial of the survival of identity after death."[3] While it is true, as this comment suggests, that many find the book "inspirational" and read it precisely as they read Bishop Fulton J. Sheen's *Peace of Soul* or Rabbi Joshua Loth Liebmann's *Peace of Mind*, it is difficult to understand how they could be misled. For, far from recommending a narcotic contemplation of the afterlife, Wilder speaks out for the vigorous pursuit of purely human relationships. If the five characters are tragic, they are so not because they die suddenly, or simply because they die, but because they have not truly lived, and at no point are we led to think that they will win the reward of an eventual reunion in heaven with the recipients of the love that for so many years enchained them. Threading through the narrative is the career of the Abbess, whose closeness to the life of Lima and attentiveness to everyday events are a reminder of the indifference of the others to such matters in their pursuit of a single goal. None of the victims escapes the measurement of his personality against that of this very vital woman. The consecration of her life to a program of work for the good of all humanity, involving her in the sacrifice of Pepita, Manuel, and Esteban, puts to shame the selfishness of the others as it is reflected in their indulgence in the anguish of love. In *The Bridge*, as in *The Cabala* and the major works which followed, Wilder insists that the life that is a rush of unanalyzed activity is as nothing when compared to the life in which the participant allows himself to become fully aware of the meaning of each experience.

Unhappily, Wilder's latter-day critics have served him

[3] Wilder to Paul Friedman, undated letter, in Friedman, "The Bridge: a Study in Symbolism," *Psychoanalytic Quarterly*, XXI (Jan. 1952), 72.

no better than his most naive readers. Impatient with the slow-moving, aphoristic style and the historical setting, they have looked back on *The Bridge* as a kind of sport among the popular novels of the 1920's and mention it as such if they mention it at all. It is true that this work contrasts bleakly with the naturalistic novels which now seem to be the sum of the literature of the decade, but to admit that fact is not to deny its quality. However much it may differ in technique from the fiction of, say, Hemingway, Fitzgerald, or John Dos Passos, it does not display a soft attitude toward the human condition. At the time of its publication it offered a considerable change in tone from the fast-paced novels of the age, and obviously a welcome change in view of the sales record, but it did not offer easy lessons in contentment.

The two volumes with which Wilder followed up the success of *The Bridge* are on the whole much less praiseworthy. It is, in fact, a matter for speculation whether *The Angel That Troubled the Waters* and *The Woman of Andros* would have found publishers if their author had not attained the status of a public figure. Although both books have merit, their quality is far from remarkable; with the closet drama and the romantic novel, the literary forms most familiar to him, Wilder had reached a point of diminishing returns.

The three-minute plays, for all the learning they reveal, are no more entertaining in the handsome format provided by Coward-McCann than in the plain pages of the *Yale Lit*. Nor, despite the experience offered by the production of *The Trumpet Shall Sound*, do the four new plays in the volume demonstrate a greater curiosity about the requirements of dramatic production than do the old ones. Like their predecessors, they are impractical for the stage because of their brevity and elaborateness. Wilder knew this, of course. What he did not recognize is that only a very few readers can interest themselves in works which deny the importance of the form they employ. The feature which most distinguishes them from the plays written in Berkeley and New Haven is not an aspect of form but a new deliberateness in the treatment of Christian values. Wilder's comment in the foreword explains his intention:

> Almost all the plays in this book are religious, but religious in that dilute fashion which is a believer's concession to a contemporary standard of good manners. But these four plant their flag as boldly as they may. It is the kind of work that I would most like to do well, in spite of the fact that there has seldom been an age in literature when such a vein was less welcome and less understood. I hope, through many mistakes, to discover the spirit that is not unequal to the elevation of the great religious themes, yet which does not fall into a repellent didacticism. (p. xv)

Accordingly, the new pieces are parables with a gentle humor in their execution. In style they are akin to *The Bridge of San Luis Rey*, and particularly the sections on the early lives of the Marquesa de Montemayor and Uncle Pio, where the sympathetic presentation of the two characters softens the tragic implications of their careers. The best of the four are *Mozart and the Gray Steward*, in which the composer learns a lesson in humility, and *The Flight into Egypt*, in which the donkey bearing the Virgin and Child receives instruction in patience and faith. But, as with all the three-minute plays, the diction falls unpleasantly on the ear, for in all but *The Flight* Wilder's piety leads him into a kind of quaintness and florid writing. Primarily a novelist still, he had not yet addressed himself seriously to the problem of creating effective dramatic prose.

The Woman of Andros, Wilder's third novel, is based on

Terence's *Andria*, but with a sufficient number of additions, deletions, and alterations to render it something more than a fictional adaptation of the play. Whereas Terence, taking his materials from late Greek comedy, had worked out a simple tale of father-son relations, set off with an instance of mistaken identity and a surprise ending that permitted all events to work out for the best in a harmonious world, Wilder built out of these materials a philosophical narrative that is not quite comedy and not quite tragedy. In Terence's play the woman of the title is Glycerium, a girl thought to be the sister of Chrysis, an Andrian courtesan, but actually the lost daughter of Chremes, an Athenian oldster. In the novel Glycerium is in fact the sister of Chrysis and therefore permanently excluded from "good" society. Her projected marriage to Pamphilus, the young scion of an important family, takes place in the novel as it does in the play, but within a few weeks of the ceremony she dies in childbirth. Although her love affair with Pamphilus and the difficulties set in the way of the marriage by old Simo, Pamphilus's father, take up the final section of the novel, Glycerium is less vital to the scheme of ideas presented by Wilder than is her sister, who, it would seem, has usurped the title part. In the wisdom of Chrysis, as she expresses her attitudes in conversation with other characters or in silent reflection, comes the first intimation of a major theme: a plea for the growth of sympathy within man for his fellow creatures.

It is in the question of each human being's regard for others that Wilder distinguishes between the pagan and Christian frames of reference. The four major adult characters of the novel, each of whom is something of an oddity or special presence in the island of Brynos (to which Wilder has moved the action from Athens), are embodiments of an inchoate Christian spirit. Chief among these is Chrysis, whose activities provide the young men of the island with an occasional opportunity for intellectual development at symposia over which she presides. She is supremely learned and supremely sophisticated, and the quality of her mind becomes apparent as she begins to demonstrate that she has somehow discovered the way to live, which is to feel moment by moment, with perfect awareness, all that life brings one's way. Impressive in her nature is a love for the world's troubled spirits, a humanitarian disposition not evident among the ordinary citizens of Brynos; in her house resides a flock of battered, distressed persons whom she sustains not only by providing them with food, clothing, and shelter, but also by providing them with love.

Within the quiet personality of Pamphilus, whose family is one of the most honored on the island, she recognizes a spirit similar to her own, and as she gains insight into his character, she begins to worry for him:

> "He thinks he is failing. He thinks he is inadequate to life at every turn. Let him rest some day, O ye Olympians, from pitying those who suffer. Let him learn to look the other way. This is something new in the world, this concern for the unfit and the broken. Once he begins that, there's no end to it, only madness. It leads nowhere. That is some god's business." Whereupon she discovered that she was weeping; but when she had dried her eyes she was still thinking about him. "Oh, such people are unconscious of their goodness. They strike their foreheads with their hands because of their failure, and yet the rest of us are made glad when we remember their faces. Pamphilus, you are another herald from the future. Some day men will be like you. Do not frown so. . . ." (pp. 77–78)

Yet the unfit and broken occupy her own thoughts much of the time.

Of all the elegants who attend her banquets, Pamphilus

is not only the most sensitive; he is much the most intelligent. He is a quiet man, seldom inclined to enter the discussions which follow her readings of literature, yet communicating his intelligence by subtle changes of facial expression. To him Wilder assigns the task of carrying into Greek society the new—almost radically new— attitude toward humanity which tempers one's judgment of the individual with sympathetic understanding of the lot of man in general. Something of his feeling for others works into the personality of the father, despite Simo's conservatism which manifests itself in the hope that Pamphilus will re-arrange his life, give up his visits to the Andrian, and marry a girl of ancient family. Simo comes to see that forces unprecedented in Greek thought are at work in his son, and he recognizes that these forces make relations between himself and the young man difficult.

To Pamphilus, as Simo gradually learns, the most admirable person on the island after Chrysis is the silent young priest of Aesculapius and Apollo, whose minis- trations to the sick, conducted with the utmost tact and sensitivity, give evidence of a regard for others as all- inclusive as his own. Tacitly, through the activities of this second contemplative man of the island, Wilder implies that the pagan priest is a prototype of the self-sacrificing Christian priest of the future. His is the quality of person- ality to which Pamphilus most quickly responds.

To point up the facets of character which Pamphilus displays early in the novel, Wilder brings about his first meeting with Glycerium at a moment when the girl is fleeing some menacing young toughs. Still later, as evidence of the growth of his feeling, Pamphilus postpones his decision to marry the girl until he can spend a day in silent meditation and fasting. Ultimately Simo, perceiving that his son is worried lest the family suffer and recognizing at last the strength of his love for the girl, sanctions the marriage. With the actions of these characters, Wilder attempts a distillation of the Christian spirit of tolerance and forbearance and for emphasis places them in a pre-Christian setting.

Like the first and second novels, *The Woman of Andros* is rooted in the conviction that a life controlled by a single drive fails to bring satisfaction. Here, however, the expression of this conviction takes a new form. Absent from the novel are personalities such as those revealed by Mlle de Morfontaine and the Marquesa de Montemayor, who while setting themselves toward one unworthy goal miss the values of the present. Approaching the subject from another direction, Wilder delivers through the ideas of Chrysis a caveat to Pamphilus and the other youths of Brynos, and hence to the reader, that for the full life they must allow themselves to enjoy each event as it happens, from the most complex down to the simplest. This warning she gives indirectly one evening by telling the company assembled in her house an anecdote of a dying hero who receives permission from Zeus to live one day of his past a second time. Required by the god to become both participant and observer on that day, the hero comes back to his old home as a boy of fifteen. But the experiment brings nothing but distress, for although he longed for the opportunity to see his parents again, he is shocked by their passivity and detachment and quickly asks to be released from life.

> "Suddenly the hero saw that the living too are dead and that we can only be said to be alive in those moments when our hearts are conscious of our treasure; for our hearts are not strong enough to love every moment. And not an hour had gone by before the hero who was both watching life and living it called on Zeus to release him from so terrible a dream. The gods heard him, but before he left he fell upon the ground and kissed the soil of the world that is too dear to be realized." (p. 36)

Nevertheless, we must make the effort to realize the world:

such is the implication of the passage, as later it was to be the implication of the same anecdote when reworked for the last act of *Our Town*. A few moments before dying, after she has made a sign to the priest to deliver her through death from the terrible pain in her side, Chrysis has a message of similar import for Pamphilus:

> "Perhaps we shall meet somewhere beyond life when all these pains shall have been removed. I think the gods have some mystery still in store for us. But if we do not, let me say now . . ." her hands opened and closed upon the cloths that covered her, ". . . I want to say to someone . . . that I have known the worst that the world can do to me, and that nevertheless I praise the world and all living. All that is, is well. Remember some day, remember me as one who loved all things and accepted from the gods all things, the bright and the dark. And do you likewise. Farewell." (p. 107)

These are admirable passages; once encountered, they stay in the mind. But they are not enough to recommend the entire novel, which remains the greatest disappointment among Wilder's extended works. It is a mixture of good and bad, with the bad prevailing. Wilder's didacticism, already overdeveloped in the first two novels, seems to have slipped quite out of control. As the tale moves along, Wilder sets out pieces of his mind on the conduct of the Christian life, but fails to illustrate his ideas suitably. For the most part the book presents a philosophical discourse without the action necessary to sustain it; we are taken into the thoughts of the characters for a direct revelation of their anxieties, but denied the satisfaction of observing those anxieties expressed through action. Moreover, Wilder offers such a scanty description of the island that it scarcely has atmosphere at all. These weaknesses cumulate in a torpid, romantic prose which takes the characters so smoothly through the pages that they seem to be floating just above ground. We could wish for at least some of the bluntness of speech which must have been heard from time to time at such banquets as Chrysis's. Though only two thirds the length of *The Cabala* or *The Bridge*, the novel bears so great a weight of humanistic speculation as to falter on nearly every page. Understandably enough, it has proved to be the least popular of the five novels Wilder has published. At the present moment it is the only one of his major works not available for mass distribution in an inexpensive, soft-bound printing.

But it is unlikely that *The Woman of Andros* will ever suffer complete neglect, for the dispute in which it figured shortly after publication has locked it into American literary history. The spark was a lengthy review of the novel and the three earlier volumes for the *New Republic* by the veteran Communist journalist Michael Gold. In his essay Gold brought down thunder on Wilder, his works, his defenders in criticism, and his public, as though to destroy all in one massive explosion. That he was hoping for a battle is sufficiently clear from the glaring contemptuousness of his title: "Wilder: Prophet of the Genteel Christ."

The style of the review is, for the *New Republic* of 1930, astonishingly hostile. Because of the piety revealed in Wilder's humanism, it was repugnant to Gold, and the novels and plays, which had not only ignored the struggle of the working class but had become increasingly distant in scene, were his natural targets. Gold complains that in failing to write of contemporary America Wilder had shown himself to be snobbish and effete, a pander, in other words, to the taste of the bourgeoisie. Looking for some recognition of the problems of workers in Wilder's books, he found only a "pastel, pastiche, dilettante religion, without the true neurotic blood and fire, a daydream of homosexual figures in graceful gowns moving archaically among the lillies. . . ."

> And is this the style [he added] with which to express America? Is this the speech of a pioneer continent? Will this discreet French drawing-room hold all the blood, horror, and hope of the world's new empire? Is this the language of the intoxicated Emerson? Or the clean, rugged Thoreau, or vast Whitman? Where are the modern streets of New York, Chicago, and New Orleans in these little novels? Where are the cotton mills and the murder of Ella May and her songs? Where are the child slaves of the beet fields? Where are the stockbroker suicides, the labor racketeers, or passion and death of the coal miners? Where are Babbitt, Jimmy Higgins, and Anita Loos's Blonde? Is Mr. Wilder a Swede or a Greek, or is he an American? No stranger would know from these books he has written.[4]

This is a calculated polemic, a deliberate affront to reason. It ignores, first, that literature may be relevant to its time without reflecting the present moment, and, second, that the struggle within the soul is no less urgent than the struggle within the body politic. Hart Crane caught Gold's tone nicely in designating the review "the recent rape of *The Woman of Andros*."[5] Wilder was not without champions after the onslaught; one of the most eminent was the fair-minded Edmund Wilson, who refused to let his sympathy for leftist causes stand in the way of a sharp reply to Gold.[6] But Gold found strong support in many quarters. For eight weeks the *New Republic* carried a spate of angry letters from both camps,

[4] Michael Gold, "Wilder: Prophet of the Genteel Christ," *New Republic*, LXIV (Oct. 22, 1930), 266.
[5] Quoted in Daniel Aaron, *Writers on the Left: Episodes in American Literary Communism* (New York: Harcourt, Brace & World, 1961), p. 242.
[6] Edmund Wilson, *The Shores of Light* (New York: Farrar, Straus and Young, 1952), pp. 502–503.

until at last, and wearily, the editors called an end to the correspondence "on account of darkness." [7]

Probably the quarrel has greater meaning as part of the record of the Communist literary movement, which reached its zenith in the late 1930's, than as an event in Wilder's career. There is no evidence in any form that the review distressed or irritated him, for wisely he made no public comment on it. Yet after the climate had cooled, he was discovered to be at work on a series of short plays with American settings, and ultimately to be composing a novel whose scenes are overcast by the Great Depression, that disaster which Gold and his fellow Communists had long predicted, and which they now hailed as the confirmation of their diagnosis of the nation's weaknesses.

[7] "Correspondence," *New Republic*, LXV (Dec. 17, 1930), 141.

IV. The American Present

THE TWO VOLUMES which Wilder published while at the University of Chicago bear so little resemblance in style and structure to his fiction of the 1920's as to seem almost the work of another man. In person, to be sure, he was much the same—as studious and as footloose as before—but in print he abandoned at last the preciosity which had marred the first novels and in 1930 had nearly caused the extinction of critical interest in his talent. Quickening to the literary possibilities of the American temperament, he left the distant, romantic scenes which formerly had fascinated him and began, with good will and an absence of satiric intent, to investigate the least sensational aspects of life at home.

It was not to be expected that on its appearance in 1931 the group of six short plays titled *The Long Christmas Dinner and Other Plays in One Act* should generate as much excitement as the novels. The public for new plays in print is always small, is smaller than usual if the plays are one-acts, and is infinitesimal if they have not been performed and reviewed. That the book was issued jointly by a commercial publisher and the Yale University

Press is a clue to the audience it was likely to reach—that is, Wilder's most dedicated readers among the general public along with his academic following. Nevertheless, the plays were Wilder's most important original work up to the date of their publication.

The six pieces sort out into two groups. Three relate to the three-minute plays of the previous decade, and three are developed in a technique then completely new to Wilder. It is a temptation to dismiss *Queens of France*, *Love and How to Cure It*, and *Such Things Only Happen in Books* as stodgy and inconsequential.[1] They suffer by comparison with the others in the volume, which for profundity and precision of expression go beyond the usual twenty- or thirty-minute performance. Yet even they represent an advance, for they are at least actable. Each is an examination of the fantasy-building strain in human nature and introduces at least one character so romantic that he is easily beguiled by others or by his own quaint disposition.

Such Things Only Happen in Books and *Love and How to Cure It* are bland but high-sounding comedies. In the former the principal character is a young novelist who has convinced himself that a grave difference exists between life and fiction. In most fiction, if not in his own, every wife has a lover, the cook serves the family's food to friends who wander into the kitchen, and murderers always return to the scene of the crime. Although such things happen in his own household, he calmly goes through life without becoming aware of them, his own sense of superiority making it impossible for him to respond intelligently to daily events. *Love and How to Cure It* presents an English undergraduate of the 1890's who is lost in love for an unresponsive music-hall dancer. He

---

[1] Wilder himself has dismissed *Such Things Only Happen in Books*. It is not included in the 1963 reprint of the volume.

cannot understand that her art, such as it is, satisfies her completely, and that his romantic dreaminess renders him unfit for love, at least in her eyes. He thinks of killing her, and when his scheme fails talks a little about killing himself. Finally he is able to give her up and to go on living, the events of the moment having been enough to satisfy his romantic soul. When all is said, it is the girl who is at fault, for she is unable to condone his passion. She is not incapable of love, but the *idea* of love is beyond her, and she cannot grasp its subtleties. Neither play is inspired; as with the three-minute pieces, Wilder did not have quite enough to say.

Less jejune than these two plays is *Queens of France*, which lacks their faintly unpleasant quality of playfulness. It is a moving account of the gulling of several women of nineteenth-century New Orleans by a charlatan who tells them, one after the other, that they are heiresses to the French throne and bilks them of their savings for funds to prove their descent from royalty. He chooses well: each of the women lives so dull a life that she is open to his fantastic suggestion. As one by one they come under his spell, they make a claim upon the sympathy of the audience, just as does the student of *Love and How to Cure It* for overestimating his adored dancer. For each of these characters, and possibly for the foolish writer of *Such Things*, Wilder requests compassion, because each is blind to the truth that life just as it is, is rich enough.

The difference between this group and the remaining three plays in the volume is more than striking. It suggests that Wilder had suddenly obtained an altogether new insight into dramatic method. Gone is the admiration for the unfamiliar and the tendency toward flowery dialogue. But these absences do not wholly explain the difference. Nor is it that the plays are expressionistic rather than naturalistic or illusionistic, though in view of his earliest efforts in drama this was a remarkable change in itself. The impressive quality is the new freedom from convention which Wilder demonstrates in the skillful manipulation of time and place.

Dramatic expressionism as developed in Germany during the first two decades of the century had conventions of its own, consisting principally of the starkness of the settings, from which most localizing details were stripped away, and the presentation of characters deliberately rendered two-dimensional for the purpose of indicating types rather than individuals. In whole or in generous part these techniques had been taken over by a few adventurous American playwrights of the 1920's—for example, by Elmer Rice in *The Adding Machine*, George S. Kaufman and Marc Connelly in *Beggar on Horseback*, and Sophie Treadwell in *Machinal*. Among the Americans, only Eugene O'Neill had experimented with a truly broad range of anti-naturalistic techniques, including not only the devices of the European expressionists, but masks, soliloquies and asides, and the use of modern colloquial dialogue for a "debunking" treatment of history. Although a few of Wilder's three-minute plays are anti-naturalistic insofar as they present situations which could not occur in life, such as animals in conversation with human beings and death in human form, none ranges altogether freely in time and space. *The Long Christmas Dinner*, *Pullman Car Hiawatha*, and *The Happy Journey to Trenton and Camden* demonstrate, through the simplification of setting and character, Wilder's awareness of the work of the expressionists at home and abroad, but they also exhibit a new and fully realized personal style.

Each of the three plays has its own way of treating the problems imposed on narrative method by the stage. In *The Long Christmas Dinner* the life of three generations of a midwestern family moves across the stage in half an hour, as wives, daughters, daughters-in-law, sons, and grandsons reveal through table conversation the passing of the years. Both *Pullman Car Hiawatha* and *The Happy Journey* make use of a figure designated "Stage Manager" who indicates the scene and moves a few pieces of furniture about, but in neither play is this character allowed to become an all-seeing, all-telling chorus whose appearances mark off periods of time. In *Pullman Car* Wilder describes a trip through time and space in the nocturnal movement of a train from New York to Chicago; the cross-country ride requires only half an hour on stage, but it is a multi-leveled experience including not only the sense of motion, but a geographical and sociological history of the territory over which the train passes. *The Happy Journey* is a daylight trip made by one family in an automobile. As they pass through New Jersey, the observant travelers bring to the attention of the audience an abundance of details of rural and urban landscapes. They hasten or slow down the passage of time merely by dwelling longer on some roadside phenomena than on others and pause at last at the end of their trip to act out a brief scene. Whereas the typical expressionistic playwrights had built up their plays on short scenes often ending in blackouts or quick curtains, Wilder in these three plays offered not one scene or a series of separate vignettes, but a flow of time, regulating the passage of the hours for specific effects of character or situation.

In the presentation of character Wilder's innovation is so subtle as to pass almost unnoticed. It is, to repeat, a simplification of character, but without the distortion of the expressionists. Unlike most anti-naturalistic dramatists, who use the actor to reveal a type by portraying not the total man but his ruling passion, Wilder tries to embody in the characters of these plays the popular concepts— "images," in the current jargon—of persons with certain definite functions to perform in life. He offers the upper-middle-class family with the members revealed in relation to one another in highly familiar ways, such as the reminiscing widow and her respectful daughter-in-law, and the spoiled son and his irate father; the lower-middle-class family, with the religious mother and her blasphemous son; the Negro Pullman porter, forever good-natured and responsive; the construction engineer, forever unintellectual; and so on, through a wide range of humanity. Clichés they may be, but because clichés issue from closely observed activity, they function well as expressions of the truths about human nature in each play. Evident, also, is the fact that Wilder has no axe to grind. The plays are not sociological tracts. They are not intended to revise our ideas about the virtues of the proletariat, the constraints of suburban living, or the horrors of repressed sexuality, though each of these matters receives attention. In short, the plays are not topical, as was most of the anti-naturalistic drama written in America and on the Continent during the 1920's. All economic classes receive careful attention, and all face the same problem: the difficulty of finding a quiet moment for calm speculation on the meaning of experience.

The very familiarity of the characters and situations elicits a strong emotional response, just as a sudden memory of a happy childhood event can sometimes induce tears. The economy of setting and gesture, spare despite the elaborateness of the occurrences depicted, enhances the bittersweetness of the theme in a way that was then quite new to Wilder. Whereas the exotic locales of the early novels and of the three-minute plays tend to drown action and thereby to dull the emotional effect, in these three pieces the bare stage stunningly sets off each phrase and lends to it a quality of primal importance, for to dispense with ornateness is to give new meaning to much that might ordinarily seem simple or drab. In *The Long Christmas Dinner* only a table, some chairs, and two portals set a play which spans ninety years of family conversation. The births and deaths of the family are indicated by the appearance or departure of characters through the portals, and the grief or joy appropriate to these events takes place at a dining-room table as the family gathers for its holiday feast. Through these displays of feeling comes the meaning of the play, for each birth or death is to this family, as to any other, the moment when the members most closely draw together and recognize the strength of their interdependence. Against this simple background the cry of the daughter Genevieve, a girl of the middle generation of the family, comes with immense force as she mourns the death of her mother: "I never told her how wonderful she was. We all treated her as though she were just a friend in the house. I thought she'd be here forever" (p. 16). It becomes the cry of everyone in grief. The repetition of births and deaths is the very meaning of the play, and on the nearly empty stage the family gives it full value by symbolizing all families everywhere, with nothing more personal to mark their specific identity than the few quirks and gestures necessary for turning table talk into dialogue.

A stage so barren of decor that it becomes as vast as the universe was not new to dramatic art when Wilder came to employ it. The stage of the English Renaissance and, to go farther back, the empty *plateae* and the pageant carts of medieval English drama had also given a sense of infinity and eternity. But the deliberate indication of all time and space *at once* was new, and it afforded Wilder many avenues of experiment. *Pullman Car Hiawatha* exploits the bare stage more fully than either of its companion pieces. As the train glides through the night, the occupants of its cars are not alone in contributing to the stage action; to point up their place in the cosmos, the ground over which they pass and the stars and planets overhead also contribute to the dialogue. The position of the car "geographically, meteorologically, astronomically, theologically" receives description. A Stage Manager, who more closely resembles a circus ringmaster than the traditional manager of an acting troupe, brings on a chorus of "hours"—young women passing over the stage with gilt numerals for the hours of the night, each speaking the words of a great philosopher. Other apparitions are a hobo riding under the train, a worker killed during the construction of the road, a watchman employed by the railway company, a mechanic well informed in meteorological lore, and the town of Grover's Corners, Ohio, represented by a schoolboy.

When these figures disappear, the angels Gabriel and Michael come on in blue serge suits to remind the audience that the car moves on its journey under the eye of a loving but mysterious God. They approach two women passengers, one who is insane and one who is tubercular. The insane woman would like to go away with these silent but smiling emissaries of God, but learns that she must stay on earth a while longer. The tubercular woman, whose death has already been reported, is the creature whom they must lead away. Unhappy with herself, believing she is not worthy to enter heaven, she asks to stay alive: "Oh, I'm ashamed! I'm just a stupid and you know it. I'm just another American" (p. 67). As she goes, she says goodbye to her childhood home, her schoolteachers, and her old friends, a little reluctant to leave as the memories of persons and places buried in memory crowd into her mind. In a minute it is morning, and the train arrives in Chicago, the passengers happy and bustling as they prepare to deboard it. Thus the trip, a very simple undertaking, is revealed to have as its background all history and all time and space. Such is the vast environment of all that we do. The play implies that the sum of man's knowledge and enterprise is the setting for each of us through life.

Less elaborate, but correspondingly more moving, is *The Happy Journey to Trenton and Camden*, with which the slim book closes. Wilder takes the Kirby family—father, mother, son, and daughter—of Newark, New Jersey, to the home in Camden of an older daughter who has just undergone the dangerous delivery of a stillborn child. Four chairs represent the car, the bare stage is the roadside, and the Stage Manager is a multitude of friendly persons encountered by the Kirbys.

The family matches so perfectly the common image of the American lower middle class that it is above any taint of caricature. Wilder's method is not satiric; nor is it purely reportorial, as if he wished only to explain to other segments of society that this is what certain neighbors of theirs are like. He speaks to that impulse which is felt by the great majority of Americans to label themselves middle class, but which is checked by a strong reluctance to own up to special privilege. The evangelical fervor of Ma Kirby is the most extreme characteristic possessed by any member of the family, but, extreme though it may be, it is not fatuous. The austerity of her belief conceals the depth of her love for her children and permits her to discipline them by chiding their natural rebelliousness, for otherwise she would simply spoil them. Pa Kirby is merely the father, responsive to his wife's wishes and hesitant to display emotion. The play is an absorbing depiction of family love, as with a superb sense of intimacy the four Kirbys enjoy the wonders of their state (including, for those in the know among the audience, a glimpse of Lawrenceville). The growing sense of warmth, generated as in the two similar plays by the simplicity of the dialogue, reaches its peak when the four travelers see the convalescent girl they have come to visit. Nothing in any of the plays surpasses the girl's question to her father: "Are you glad I'm still alive, pa?" (p. 120). Into this line, composed of some of the homeliest words in the language, Wilder packs three of man's basic feelings: the desire for love, the fear of rejection, and the fear of death. At the moment of the play's conclusion comes the tacit suggestion that all will be well for the entire family, and, consequently, for all humanity.

In December 1934 *Heaven's My Destination* was published in England; the first American edition followed at the beginning of the new year. According to Wilder, the title comes from "Doggerel verse which children of the Middle West were accustomed to write in their schoolbooks." He printed the verse in full along with the explanation on the title page, supplying names from the novel:

> *George Brush* is my name;
> America's my nation;
> *Ludington's* my dwelling-place
> And Heaven's my destination.

Although it was largely ignored when first printed, the book now emerges as Wilder's most substantial fiction and one of the strongest American novels of the 1930's. The setting for once is no remote, exciting, or idyllic territory, but the American Midwest from the late summer of 1930 to the late summer of 1931. The land is drab and gray, drained of life by the market crash and seemingly irredeemable. Yet it is not the depiction of the depression scene which gives the novel its strength, for the details are few. *Heaven's My Destination* is not the answer to Michael Gold's plea for a novel on working-class necessities. It does not give that icy feeling of sudden impoverishment much depression fiction projects; for only one example, John Steinbeck's *The Grapes of Wrath* offers a more profoundly unsettling picture of economic distress. Nor is Wilder militant. He tells nothing whatever of the life of the unemployed masses. For the revolutionary spirit we should have to turn to the self-styled "proletarian" fiction of the decade in which it is sometimes competently presented, as in the novels of Jack Conroy and Josephine Herbst. The value of the work lies elsewhere. It is in the portrait of an American who represents the majority of his countrymen at the same time that he is a special, and specially moving, figure. Like the three one-act plays, the novel addresses that quality of the American mind which tends to isolate and identify certain points of view, patterns of movement, and rhythms of speech as middle class and native, regardless of time, place, and economic conditions.

In his *Paris Review* interview of 1956 Wilder commented frankly on the forces other than those present in the sunken economy which moved him to write the novel. His twenty-three-year-old hero, George Brush, resembles himself as a young man in his hardheaded Calvinism and, what is more, attended a college in which that severe mode of belief prevailed among the student body, as it did at Oberlin. The novel, then, is his attempt to "come to terms" with the influences active upon him in youth.[2] He has observed privately that Brush is drawn not only from his own life, but from the personalities of his father and brother, and that lightly covering these is his memory of yet another seeker after the light, Gene Tunney.[3] The struggle against the bonds of evangelical religion is thus

[2] Richard H. Goldstone, "Thornton Wilder," in *Writers at Work: The Paris Review Interviews*, ed. Malcolm Cowley (New York: Viking Press, 1958), p. 104.

[3] Isabel Wilder.

the primary matter of the novel, and the depression setting is the field on which it takes place. It is a particularly American struggle, since in no other country do the evangelical sects have such popularity. The midwestern "Bible belt" is their most fertile territory.

The freedom to move about at will across the vastness of the nation is also deeply ingrained in American life, and the temptation to take advantage of it has acted as a constant goad to Americans since the earliest explorations of the continent. It is true that we cannot claim the invention of the railroad, but we have given the world the automobile and the airplane and have put them to such fantastic use that we are known to be the most mobile people on earth. It may be remembered that at the time of the writing of *Heaven's My Destination* the trailer— since dignified as the "mobile home"—came into its own; its advantage was that it permitted the owner to retain all the comforts of domesticity while roaming as he pleased. It is, then, much to the point that in Wilder's only fiction set in America the hero should be that harried, joked about, yet ordinary American white-collar wage-earner, the traveling salesman, and that his very life should be an enactment of one of the most repeated jokes, the joke everybody knows about the traveling salesman and the farmer's daughter. Once we recognize the familiar story, we may not wish to admit our kinship with Brush, but he is one of us all the same.

In giving scope to Brush's activities, Wilder adopted a style free of hyperliterary adornment for the first time in his fiction. It is precisely right for a plot of such homeliness. Abandoning completely the aphoristic technique, he uses a plain, descriptive prose and refrains from imposing philosophical observations upon it. Consequently, ideas emerge from the action alone, and we are not prodded toward a particular viewpoint by the comments of an omniscient narrator. Dialogue composes much more of the bulk than in the first three novels, and its idiom is the common currency of everyday American speech. Through colloquialisms which impart a sense of spontaneity, it skillfully catches the inelegance of middle-class life. It is the language of the ordinary human being who is usually too bewildered to compose graceful sentences. The style is especially effective for those parts of the novel in which Brush tries to express his highly personal ideas of conduct. In the following passage, his first long speech, we hear him struggling, with just enough words at his command, to explain to the president of a bank why he must withdraw all the money in his account. Only the reasons are unusual, not the diction.

> "Why, I'm glad to tell you Mr. Southwick. You see, I've been thinking about money and banks a lot lately. I haven't quite thought the whole matter through yet— I'll be able to do that when my vacation comes in November—but at least I see that for myself I don't believe in saving money any more. Up till now I used to believe that you were allowed to save *some* money—like five hundred dollars, for instance, for your old age, you know, or for the chance your appendix burst, or for the chance you might get married suddenly—for what people call a rainy day; but now I see that's all wrong. I've taken a vow, Mr. Southwick; I've taken the vow of voluntary poverty." (pp. 20–21)

As we listen he slowly pays out his phrases in the hope of receiving a nod of comprehension, and at last manages to say it all.

The man who speaks these words is a recognizable figure. He has the middle-class virtues of gregariousness, fastidiousness, and helpfulness in great abundance; and along with them he has one familiar fault: a tendency to mistake his prejudices for reasoned opinions. But in

Wilder's delineation of Brush is much that is not so recognizable, and in this the man's personality takes on the color that gives the novel its value. As Brush bumps along the route assigned him by the textbook company for which he works, he fights constantly against troubles originating in the unexplored core of his being. Shackled to the fundamentalism preached to him in his late teens by a drug-addicted girl evangelist, and further bound by four years of indoctrination at Shiloh Baptist College in South Dakota, Brush antagonizes everyone whose path crosses his, with the exception of a humorous judge who takes a moment to pity him. Nobody has ever liked him, despite his generosity, his attractive physique, and his good tenor voice, and without realizing it, he is badly in need of affection. Were he *consciously* hostile, he would be grotesque; but, giving offense while doing his best to be helpful, he is pathetic. Brush works hard to form relationships, only to let each of them go once he hears an opinion from the person in question contrary to a conviction of his own. He is said to be "good as gold" (p. 279), and with justification, since he prevents a suicide, gives money away almost continuously, makes a home for an orphan, and sends a young woman through college—all without the expectation of a return. But the unalterable narrowness of his character so gravely threatens his well-being that in addition to love he needs protection from himself. As he travels, his eyes and ears are open for the farmer's daughter, who he believes is yoked to him forever in a spiritual union; but the search is delayed by fights, jailings, and rough house, as well as by his frequent displays of kindliness. He moves through his scenes haltingly, not conquering his problems, but becoming more deplorably tormented by them as the year passes.

It is true that Wilder has put much into Brush's character of which he approves, along with the dismaying stubbornness. Brush's quarrels, no matter what form they take, are conflicts between spirituality and materialism. With few exceptions, the persons who come up against his armored innocence are still clinging to the values of the boom years, that period in American life which from the vantage point of the 1930's seemed to have undercut all moral principles. From incident to incident, tension rises as Brush, with his obvious, admitted disapproval of wealth, moves into situations where money determines the rules of behavior. It is not, we have seen, through fear that Southwick's bank will fail that he draws out his savings, but through the utter certainty of conviction that to possess money at all is to be guilty of a grave offense. Southwick's arguments, which have to do with fiscal matters and are given urgency by his worries for the bank, cannot touch him. Saved from alarm by his own sense of rectitude, he blandly observes after the police intervene, "I didn't do anything. I just told a bank president that banks were immoral places and they arrested me" (p. 26). The tone of the scene is comic, as in most of Brush's dealings with humanity, but not light-hearted. It does not conceal the sense that although Brush's principles are based on Christian morality and are therefore admirable in themselves, his hope of changing the world by his own example in living up to them cannot succeed in the materialistic, irreligious America of this century.

His second arrest in the novel results from another comic situation, but ends in a deeply felt incident. At this time, in order to act upon another of his beliefs, he assists a holdup man in robbing an elderly woman shopkeeper. Brush holds firmly to Mahatma Gandhi's theory of *ahimsa*, the idea that passive resistance to one's enemy will conquer him by effecting a change in his social attitudes. Knowing that Mrs. Efrim, the shopkeeper, hides her money under a bolt of cloth, he points it out to the young hoodlum, who has expressed fury over finding no more than two dollars and a quarter in the till. Like the scene in the bank, this episode leads to laughter, despite the distress of the woman and the gun of the thief. But its meaning is grave; again Brush is adopting a position at odds with normality. Through sheer luck, he captures the gun and therewith gains control of the situation, but, despite his victory, he is not satisfied to turn the thief over to the police. The dictates of *ahimsa* require him to give the thief money after all, and then to set him free. He does not succeed wholly, however, for Wilder cannot lose his readers by letting the woman be robbed, and will not miss the opportunity to press home the meaning of Brush's conduct once he is brought to trial for abetting the criminal. By degrees the judge is impressed as Brush explains the theory of *ahimsa*, and Brush is soon released. But at the close of the scene the judge gives him some advice in practical behavior which he desperately requires:

> Judge Carberry put his hand on Brush's shoulder and stopped him. Brush stood still and looked at the ground. The judge spoke with effort:
> "Well, boy ... I'm an old fool, you know ... in the routine, in the routine. ... Go slow; go slow. See what I mean? I don't like to think of you getting into any unnecessary trouble. ... The human race is pretty stupid. ... Doesn't do any good to insult 'm. Go gradual. See what I mean?"
> "No," said Brush, looking up quickly, puzzled.
> "Most people don't like ideas. Well," he added, clearing his throat, "if you get into any trouble, send me a telegram, see? Let me see what I can do."
> Brush didn't understand any of this. "I don't know what you mean by trouble," he said. "But thanks a lot, Judge." (p. 247)

Two other encounters are especially effective for the exploration of Brush's complex character; one, near the opening, is set in somewhat comic tones, but the second, near the close of the novel, projects a grimly sober mood. In the early incident, Brush meets an attractive young woman named Jessie Mayhew at a holiday camp where she is working for the summer. He likes her at once, and would enjoy spending an evening with her, for, like him, she is a midwesterner, has not known special privilege, and has attended a small college. But difficulties quickly rise: he discovers that she believes in evolution and sees nothing outrageous in cigarettes for women. The girl, shaken by the meeting, can do nothing in the face of his steely opinions except spare herself the anguish of further incidents with him. By the time he meets George Burkin, Brush has experienced many such moments, and has begun to suspect at last that something is wrong. Burkin, a film director, is arrested as a Peeping Tom, and shares Brush's cell in Judge Carberry's jail. The two are released at the same time and head across country in Burkin's car. Like the judge and Jessie Mayhew, Burkin believes in compromise, but he differs from the girl in his out-spokenness. "You're the damnedest prig I ever saw. You're a bag of wind" (p. 259): these are the severest words of condemnation yet offered to Brush, and, even recognizing the cynicism in Burkin's moral constitution and knowing with all the more certainty that his own strict code of behavior is best, he feels the tears spring to his eyes. For a while he continues to ride with Burkin, but he soon decides that he must strike out alone, as always, and leaves the car in the middle of the night. Brush's spiritual journey has taken him nowhere at all.

Along with the resentment of his stubbornness which Jessie Mayhew, Burkin, and all his other acquaintances feel, come charges that Brush is out of his mind. Such unwillingness to compromise with the way of the world as he expresses is not invariably the evidence of derangement, however, and Wilder does not intend us to think of Brush as a madman. But he is deeply neurotic, a fact apparent in his repetition of a pattern of behavior which gives him no pleasure, but which he cannot escape. Like the Cabalists and the victims of the bridge, his mind is on a distant goal—the reformation of society and the marriage with the farmer's daughter which will betoken the start of it—when he should be finding enjoyment in the present moment. He responds with delight to pretty girls and to praise for his singing voice, but the slightest suggestion of a weakening in the flesh distresses him, and his voice is "just a thing of nature, like any other" (p. 40), not a possession to be exploited for gain. He carries a copy of *King Lear* with him at all times (Gene Tunney!), but on every reading he finishes the play "without discovering a trace of talent in it" (p. 119). Lacking a normal emotional life, he usually substitutes for profound feeling the exhilaration of the evangelical believer, writing Biblical texts on hotel blotters and telling the astonished passengers of railroad cars that cigarettes are an abomination. Nothing can break down his resistance to life.

Wilder underscores Brush's difficulties by crediting him with one intense desire: a longing for "a fine American home" (p. 277). Although this phrase is an obvious borrowing from the jargon of the George F. Babbitt variety of real-estate salesman, its use in the novel is not altogether satiric. The values of home life are, after all, decent and sound; it is only Brush's words that justify raillery, not his hope. But even the words transcend burlesque, for they impart to Brush that touch of pathos present in the character of all harmless but disturbed individuals. His desire for a home is essentially the desire to enter ordinary human society, and that is a step no person so self-absorbed can make without a far-reaching revision of personality. Ultimately he finds Roberta, the farmer's daughter, and persuades her to marry him. The task is not easy, however; it requires the most convincing language that he and the girl's sympathetic sister Lottie can manage. The speech which Wilder assigns to Brush for his proposal is exceptionally moving, for it is a compilation of familiar, cherishable images. But even here Brush holds back something of himself, as though not fully willing to entrust his entire personality to the girl:

> He took her hand and said: "It's going to be fine, Roberta. You'll see. What you want will always be the first thing in my mind. At first, though, I'll have to be away a good deal on the road, but I'll write you a letter every day. Later I think I can get the firm to give me the Illinois and Ohio territory. We're going to have a wonderful life together . . . you'll see. There'll be lots of times when we'll be laughing a lot . . . while we're washing the dishes, and so on . . . and soon we'll have a little house of our own. I'm very good at fixing things, like electric lights and furnaces. And I'm good at carpentering, too. I'll build you an arbor in the back yard where you can sit and sew. And Lottie can come and stay with us as long as she wants to. We could never find a better friend than Lottie. . . . Don't you think it sounds . . . like it'll be fine?"
>
> Roberta, standing with lowered eyes, said, "Yes."
>
> "I know I'm kind of funny in some ways," he added, smiling, "but that's only these earlier years when I'm trying to think things out. By the time I'm thirty all that kind of thing will be clearer to me, and . . . and it'll all be settled." (pp. 280–281)

The trouble is that Brush does not understand how small a part love plays in his plan to establish a home. Much as he might wish it, he does not love Roberta, and, unbearably honest man that he is, does not pretend to. The end is disaster: the girl cannot stand him and insists on a separation.

From his description of the collapse of the marriage, Wilder moves to a last examination of Brush's neurotic pattern. The immediate result to him of Roberta's withdrawal, coming on Burkin's denunciation, is the loss of his faith, which had provided the impetus to the marriage. This event is symbolized by his purchase of a pipe and some tobacco. Next go his perfect health and strength, and in Texas he enters a hospital with so many ailments that it seems certain he will die. What saves him is the gift of a silver spoon from a Roman Catholic priest, Father Pasziewski, who, Brush hears, has recently died after a long illness. The priest had been the friend and spiritual adviser of Queenie Craven, the proprietress of a boarding house in Kansas City where Brush keeps a room. Brush had never met Father Pasziewski, but had inquired considerately about his health on each meeting with Queenie. Although his inquiries had begun out of mere politeness, during the course of the novel they become more urgent, for the priest takes on a mystical importance in Brush's life. He too is a dedicated person, and yet people love him—the reason, of course, is that he not only preaches to men, but expresses sympathetic understanding of them. Grasping at the notion that this admired man respects him, but never pronouncing the notion aloud, Brush recovers quickly from his diseases. Soon he is his old self again in every unfortunate way, and his favorite Biblical texts reappear on the blotters of midwestern hotels.

Heaven's My Destination thus concludes pessimistically, for we have no hope for Brush. Forever invincible, he is by definition a comic hero, but when all is said there is nothing funny in the thought of his continuing the restless travels around the circle of his textbook route, never settling in the home he longs for, and never experiencing that efflorescence of personality which might enable him to find love. Yet, however much we may be put off by the final pages, the novel explores more tellingly than its predecessors in Wilder's work the failure of dogmatism and the perils lying ahead in the blind, groove-gouging life, because it includes nothing alien to twentieth-century experience. There, but for slight differences in temperament, go most of us.

In the perspective of time it is possible to detect the causes of the novel's failure with its first readers. In the mid-1930's it had no natural audience. If as an answer to the Marxists it was less then they had asked of Wilder, it was also more, for their own dogma could be substituted for Brush's fundamentalism without disturbing the theme. For those less doctrinaire readers who had enjoyed the settings Wilder had previously shown them, the depression landscape had no allure. Nor did the novel offer, for compensation, the toughness of naturalistic fiction; a few scenes of rough-house antics and practical jokes among Brush and his fellow lodgers at Queenie's are the only concessions to readers who preferred the Hemingway-Faulkner tone. And although the novel has sometimes been compared to Sinclair Lewis's *Elmer Gantry*,[4] clearly the admirers of Lewis's fiction could find little in Wilder to satisfy them. Between Brush and Gantry lie such broad differences on all systems of conduct and belief that the comparison does not hold. Brush's story is a record of the internal causes of misery that is given cogency by its very familiarity, not a free-swinging exposé of hidden vice delivered by Lewis to a cynical, aggrieved portion of the

[4] See Rex Burbank, *Thornton Wilder* (New York: Twayne Publishers, 1961), pp. 72–73.

reading public. As we follow Brush across the prairie, we are in a different world from those known to the naturalists, the proletarians, and the early Wilder. Now that the depression has receded into history, we are free to observe Brush in the clear outline of Wilder's prose, another, and the most impressive, of his cautionary fictional heroes.

V. Three Plays of the
Human Adventure

AFTER THE PUBLICATION of *Heaven's My Destination* Wilder made up his mind to write no more fiction. The decision did not come as a result of the poor showing of the novel, he later insisted, but from a growing dissatisfaction with narrative technique: he had become uncomfortably conscious of his "editorial presence." By this he meant the prodding and emphasizing of theme from an all-seeing, all-knowing position.[1] To the extent that it is possible to do so and still convey ideas, he had written George Brush's saga without the kind of direct commentary which shapes the reader's opinion of the events and assists toward an interpretation. But, still not satisfied, he turned to the form which at least seemed to prohibit a sense of the author's presence. In drama the author does not hover over the personalities of the characters, cannot point directly to those of their traits which express the meaning of the play, and is, in fact, expected to make his revelations

[1] Ross Parmenter, "Novelist into Playwright," *Saturday Review of Literature*, XVIII (June 11, 1938), 10–11.

through action and dialogue alone. Gertrude Stein had taught him that "you should talk to yourself in your own private language and be willing to sink or swim on the hope that your private language has nevertheless sufficient correspondence with that of persons of some reading and experience." [2] From 1937 to 1943 in accordance with this principle he wrote and brought to Broadway *Our Town*, *The Merchant of Yonkers*, and *The Skin of Our Teeth*.

Wilder was no stranger to the New York theater before the opening of *Our Town*. His prior record had included three productions: the off-Broadway presentation of his *The Trumpet Shall Sound* in 1926, the unsuccessful Broadway showing of André Obey's *Lucrece* in 1932 in his translation, and Jed Harris's highly praised staging of his translation of Ibsen's *A Doll's House* in 1937, also on Broadway. The list is not extensive, but together the three experiences offered a hint of what was to come with a major Broadway production of a piece entirely his own.

For the second time he worked with Harris, a thoroughly trained man of the theater whose abundant charm often gave way before an iron determination to secure the production values which would insure a run. As was typical of him, he drove and quarreled with Wilder during rehearsals, but, after a difficult tryout period, proved the soundness of his judgment with a successful production. A few preliminary performances given in Princeton went very well and seemed to augur good fortune, but in Boston, where it was scheduled for two weeks, the play was roundly damned. Since the Boston audience is no more discriminating that the Princeton or New York audience despite the traditional claim of every city that it is the most difficult to please, the future of *Our Town* was beyond prediction in the last days

[2] *Loc. cit.*

before the opening. Harris therefore decided to cut his
losses and bring in the play one week ahead of schedule.
To do so, it was necessary for him to make an interim
booking of a temporarily vacant house for *one night only*,
February 4, 1938, after which, if all went well, he would
lease another theater for the run of the play.[3]

The result was what Harris had hoped: the play caught
on at once, ran through the season and into November of
the next, and won a second Pulitzer Prize for Wilder.
Since the end of the Broadway run it has been produced
almost nightly in community and college theaters across
America, with a financial reward to the author of $400,000
as of the end of 1963.[4] It has been filmed (with most of
the cast of the Broadway production) and has been
televised twice, the second time in a musical version.
Although Harris has been eager to say that it lost money
for him in San Francisco and Los Angeles as well as in
Boston,[5] the New England metropolis is in fact the only
American city to have withheld approval. Abroad also,
as *Unsere Kleine Stadt* or *Notre petite ville*, it has held the
stage, although at its London debut in 1946, again under
Harris's direction, the play did not take. At the time of the
present writing *Our Town* has earned a position as a
classic more secure than has been accorded any other
work in the American repertory, the international
reputation of Eugene O'Neill notwithstanding.

At the beginning of the 1930's Wilder planted the seed
which was to give growth to this remarkably successful
play. The sceneryless one-acts of 1931 are the source of
its form, of the employment of the Stage Manager-
conférencier, of certain details of dialogue, and of the name

[3] Jed Harris, *Watchman, What of the Night?* (New York: Doubleday,
1963), pp. 79–81.
[4] Louis Calta, "Amateur Rights Help Dramatists," New York *Times*,
January 31, 1964, p. 17.
[5] Harris, p. 84.

of the town, Grover's Corners, where the action unfolds. From *Pullman Car Hiawatha* comes the notion of presenting the historical and sociological background, a device of importance to the expression of theme in both works, and from the same play comes the young heroine's heartfelt series of farewells to remembered scenes of happiness at the time of her death. From *The Long Christmas Dinner* come her touching but overdue words of praise for her mother. The central material of the third act, the heroine's return to life for a repetition of one day of childhood, has, it will be remembered, an earlier source in *The Woman of Andros*. In borrowing from his own writing for works of ever-broadening scope, Wilder had revealed his capacity for growth with each new publication since *The Cabala*. Yet in no work before *Our Town* had he shown such an amazing spring forward.

Behind the new development, enhancing the vision already present and opening new reaches of his imagination, stood the brilliant teaching of Gertrude Stein. The shaping of the details of the one-act plays into a comprehensive dramatic structure was Wilder's own achievement, but within his design the strength of Miss Stein's thought is apparent. The reader with the patience to work through the odd corners of the Steinian style will discover Wilder's debt to the two groups of papers delivered in 1934–1935, *Lectures in America* and *Narration*, in which the expatriate writer, having come home again, defines and accounts for the differences between the English and the American approaches to life and literature. She does not do the job well, but underneath her interminably repetitious phrasing are sound, seriously intended general notions of national characteristics. The English, she observes, are the inhabitants of an island and experience a confining "island life," whereas the Americans dwell on a continent and for that reason have developed

patterns of thought which range more widely than those
of the English. The more difficult, and correspondingly
less rewarding, *Geographical History of America* extends this
slightly to make a distinction between the minds not only
of islanders and continentals, but between valley dwellers
and plains dwellers; and America to Miss Stein was a
great continent of plains. In the same book she adds
other ideas which take up the relation of the individual
to eternity and infinity; in particular, she expresses the
notion that the mind wishes to move beyond the limits of
the individual personality and to develop a sense of all
periods of time, past, present, and future, in combination.
The ideas of the two volumes of lectures are more absorbing than those of the long and complex book, which offers
rewards only to the most dedicated of Miss Stein's
followers. But if we give the seemingly commonplace
observation on the "island life" the attention it deserves,
we will see, not only that its implications are extensive,
but that it is reflected in every facet of Wilder's play.

One effect of the geography of their native territory
upon islanders is to cause them to fall back upon themselves. Cut off from the mainland, they give thought to
little beyond their private, day-to-day existence. This is a
relationship of cause and effect which, we should note,
is as evident an influence on the life of the residents of
Nantucket or Jamaica or Manhattan as on the life of the
English; because of it, all islanders have a limited sense
of time. And not being able to move great distances by
easy means of transportation, they also have a limited
sense of space. The result to their literature is a particu-
larizing quality, a tendency to focus closely on local
scenes and issues, and an avoidance of sweeping movement. But among Americans who live on the mainland—
in effect, among all the major elements of the population
except New Yorkers—the time-space sense is powerful,

and equally powerful is the sense of mobility. We tend to view ourselves in relation to the universe, not in isolation from it, and our literature, according to Gertrude Stein, illustrates this quality of our thought. Now, it is true enough that students of the literature of England can call to mind a long list of novels and plays whose characters sail the seas or, if trapped at home, roam in fantasy. Yet Miss Stein is right to imply that American writers are much less concerned with the intimate and familiar than are the English; when an American novel describes in detail the life of one limited area, it is given the special label of *regional* fiction to account for, and often to excuse, its small compass. She is also right to imply that movement is essential to the American writer. To support her opinions, we can summon the mass of nineteenth-century American fiction to which movement is all-important to theme: for example, James Fenimore Cooper's *Leatherstocking Tales*, Harriet Beecher Stowe's *Uncle Tom's Cabin*, Mark Twain's *Huckleberry Finn*, and Herman Melville's novels of the sea, or the works which contrast the American abroad with European nationals, such as the fiction of Henry James. For closer consideration, it is sufficient to recall the most impressive novels of any single decade: for the 1930's, Fitzgerald's *Tender Is the Night*, Steinbeck's *The Grapes of Wrath*, and Wilder's own *Heaven's My Destination*. For these works it is impossible to find English equivalents, with the possible exception of Elizabeth Bowen's *To the North*. Quiet play that it is, *Our Town* reflects the Steinian comments in such depth that it reads and acts as though intended to be a systematic exposition of them in dramatic form.

Although the play begins and ends in one precisely described place, Grover's Corners, New Hampshire, it ranges far beyond the village boundaries in each of its three acts. By eliminating scenery and props, except for

two small trellises to appease persons who cannot do
without scenery, Wilder avoids from the outset any
suggestion that the *meaning* of the action relates only to
Grover's Corners, and yet, through the dialogue and the
expository remarks of the Stage Manager, he retains
enough of the New England flavor to remind the audience
of the starting point, so to speak, of the nation in which it
lives. He begins, then, in the small New England town
and from it moves out to embrace all creation. The time-
span of the play runs from 1901 to 1913, a period recent
enough in 1938 to appeal to the memory of the audience,
but still distant enough to be free of restrictive contemporary associations.

The plot is the story of two neighboring households, the
Gibbs and Webb families. Their lives are in no way
sensational or special; nothing has happened to them that
might set them off either as heroes or as victims. True,
the family heads are professional men—*Dr.* Gibbs and
Editor Webb—but the distinction implied in the titles
serves only to confer upon them a degree of familiarity
with human problems, and this they are able to communicate to the audience. As one device out of many to link
Grover's Corners to the great world beyond, Wilder also
gives the two men distinctive hobbies: Dr. Gibbs devotes
all his spare time to studies of the Civil War, and Editor
Webb is equally fascinated by the life of Napoleon.
Like its principal families, the town itself, considered as a
place on the map, possesses a distinguishing but unaston-
ishing "background," as described by local authorities:
so many members of each religious denomination live
in it, the ground under it was founded in such-and-such
geological eras, the birth and death rates are thus and so.
The purpose of this quite ordinary information is not to
particularize the town; rather, it serves to underline the
fact that Grover's Corners, the home of the Gibbses and

the Webbs, is just another spot in the cosmos. But at the same time that it is a place of no importance, the town represents the universe, and whatever occurs to its inhabitants is an expression, in very general terms, of the chief events in the lives of all people.

The scenes devised by Wilder are moments of eternity singled out for our attention and played against the panorama of infinity. The first act is titled "The Daily Life," and offers such details as the early-morning milk delivery, the family breakfast, and the children's departure for school. Proceeding from dawn till bedtime, at every turn the action distills poignance from the commonplace, including even so unremarkable an occurrence as the children's struggle with homework. In choosing this title for the act, Wilder would seem for the moment to ignore the remarks of Gertrude Stein, who said that the Americans have no daily life in the sense that the English have one—that is, that we do not think as a nation in terms of a simple, unchanging routine. But the phrase and the routine activities covered by it are useful to Wilder insofar as they carry the notion that these New Englanders, engaged as they are in ordinary, mundane duties, are authentic representatives of the entire race. Similarly, the titles of the second and third acts, "Love and Marriage" and "Death," the latter only hinted at, not explicitly given, describe the fundamental material of existence.

Of the twenty-two characters who pass across the stage, most are present only to populate the arena whose principal actors are George Gibbs and Emily Webb, the older children of the two families. Through the conduct of their lives, which, as we see them on Wilder's bare stage, they lead in infinite space at a point in the endless continuum of time, emerges in little the general pattern of the human adventure. At the moments when they act out their personal joy and sadness, they present an abstract rendering of these emotions as they come to us all. They are allegorical figures, but, because what they represent is not a special quality or force but the complete sum of the human passions, and because also they speak in an ordinary manner without the aggrandizing self-consciousness of an Everyman, they are completely absorbing as characters in their own right. In attending, as it were, to the development of George and Emily, Wilder is concerned primarily with their virtues, but he does not omit the vices from the design of their personalities. Thus, for example, they delight in ice cream sodas, delay over their homework, and plan ahead for a profitable farm. These interests are nothing less than the deadly sins of gluttony, sloth, and avarice, yet so softened as to round out the design without rendering the boy and girl egregious. The point is that if we are to see ourselves in George and Emily, we must not be so dismayed that we avert our eyes. The two protagonists grow up in houses on adjacent properties, play together as children, fall in love with one another in adolescence, and marry as soon as they graduate from high school. Emily dies in childbirth after nine years of marriage, and as the play ends George grieves hopelessly beside her grave. That is all. But so basic to the life of every civilization are these experiences and the emotions they evoke that their theatrical impact is universally stunning.

To extend the dimensions of the plot, Wilder employs images of vast numbers which with a lightly comic tone the Stage Manager pulls out of his capacious mind. In three years the sun comes up a thousand times, in long marriages husbands and wives may eat as many as fifty thousand meals together, every bride and groom have millions of ancestors, all of whom may be spectral guests at the wedding. To take the audience out of the present moment and move the play forward in time, Wilder permits the Stage Manager to use his omniscience in still another way: he mentions not only the past and present of the characters' lives, but their future, including, for many, the dates and circumstances of their deaths. At the end of the first act, after we have listened at length to his observations, we come to understand through the words of another figure, George Gibbs's young sister Rebecca, that over all dates and places and activities such as we have been hearing of, God eternally watches:

> REBECCA: I never told you about that letter Jane Crofut got from her minister when she was sick. The minister of her church in the town she was in before she came here. He wrote Jane a letter and on the envelope the address was like this: It said: Jane Crofut; The Crofut Farm; Grover's Corners; Sutton County; New Hampshire; United States of America.
> GEORGE: What's funny about that?
> REBECCA: But listen, it's not finished: the United States of America; Continent of North America; Western Hemisphere; the Earth; the Solar System; the Universe; the Mind of God—that's what it said on the envelope.
> GEORGE: What do you know!
> REBECCA: And the postman brought it just the same.
> GEORGE: What do you know! (pp. 54–55)

Closely related to Gertrude Stein's comments on the generalizing tendency of Americans, this scene, in which the life of Grover's Corners in all its pedestrian details has become the focus of cosmic forces, nevertheless projects a quality which is pure Wilder. Each act contains a moment of beauty and pathos, and of great familiarity, which moves the play forward with a sureness of theatrical technique obviously beyond the ability of Miss Stein to inspire. In the first act it is a scene between George and his father in which the boy is scolded mildly for letting his mother chop wood for the stove when he should be doing the job himself. In the second act it is the acute bridal fear of Emily immediately before the wedding ceremony as she expresses it in an anguished plea to George: "Well, if you love me, help me. All I want is someone to love me" (p. 94). In the last, it is Emily's brief, emotionally harrowing return to life and a re-enactment of her fourteenth birthday. Unable to communicate with her family and suddenly aware that in the entire process of her life the minutes have passed too quickly to be fully realized, she cannot endure the massive grief now developing:

> EMILY: (*In a loud voice to the* STAGE MANAGER.) I can't. I can't go on. Oh! Oh! It goes too fast. We don't have time to look at one another. (*She breaks down sobbing. At a gesture from the* STAGE MANAGER, MRS. WEBB *disappears.*) I didn't realize. So all that was going on and we never noticed. Take me back—up the hill—to my grave. But first: Wait! One more look. Good-by. Good-by, world. Good-by, Grover's Corners... Mama and Papa. Good-by to clocks ticking... and Mama's sunflowers. And food and coffee. And new-ironed dresses and hot baths... and sleeping and waking up. Oh, earth, you're too wonderful for anybody to realize you. (*She looks toward the* STAGE MANAGER *and asks abruptly, through her tears:*) Do any human beings realize life while they live it?—every, every minute?
> STAGE MANAGER: No. (*Pause.*) The saints and poets, maybe—they do some. (pp. 124–125)

With this scene we come to a point to which Wilder always directs us: the belief that the cause of man's unhappiness is not his failure to achieve or sustain greatness, but his failure to delight in the beauty of ordinary existence. In the preface to his *Three Plays*, the collected edition of his major dramatic works, he writes forthrightly of this theme:

> *Our Town* is not offered as a picture of life in a New
> Hampshire Village; or as speculation about the con-
> ditions of life after death (that element I merely took
> from Dante's *Purgatory*). It is an attempt to find a value
> above all price for the smallest events in our daily
> life. . . . Molière said that for the theatre all he needed
> was a platform and a passion or two. The climax of this
> play needs only five square feet of boarding and the
> passion to know what life means to us. (pp. xii–xiii)

The people of Grover's Corners are the sort whose effect
upon the world is slight, slighter even than the effect of
such a man as George Brush, since they never move away
from their particular piece of the universe. For that reason
they are the personages whose lives most clearly reflect
the marvelousness of the unheroic.

Wilder's choice of New England for the setting
strengthens the play to the extent, as we have observed,
that a depiction of fundamental passions may be especially
moving to an American audience if the scene itself is
fundamentally and simply American. In this regard, no
region qualifies so well as does the birthplace of the nation.
On the other hand, nothing vital would be lost if the
setting were changed to any other uncomplicated community; in 1962 *Life* illustrated the play very satisfactorily
with a series of photographs of a small town in South
Dakota where it had recently been performed.[6] For that
matter, Rome, Lima, the Greek islands, and the American
Midwest had served Wilder as backgrounds against which
to project the same theme, though none had proved quite
so successful as the New Hampshire village. For Wilder's
purposes in the play, the uniquely indispensable characteristic of the community's populace is its colloquial
speech. Familiar everywhere in the nation, it possesses
the quality which Wilder admired in Gertrude Stein's

6 "The Abiding Truths of 'Our Town,'" *Life*, LIII (Sept. 7, 1962), 52–67.

Narration. In his preface to the book he described it as coming from the "daily life." [7] Before Wilder, writers had refrained from using it in tragedy out of fear of lowering the tone, or, like O'Neill in *Desire Under the Elms*, had buttressed it with regional idioms.

That the play is a tragedy, despite the simplicity of the dialogue, is beyond dispute, for we see the death of Emily cutting short the happiness which the young protagonists had earned by the conduct of their lives. Their distress brings the reminder that no amount of effort to achieve honor and dignity such as theirs will confer immortality. The only mitigating notion lies in Emily's urgent lament for the lost opportunity to enjoy simple pleasures. The wisest onlookers will respond to the implicit warning of her last speeches and make what use of it they can. Possibly it will function in their lives to increase their own awareness. Yet it is true that the theme is equally suitable for comedy, as Wilder had demonstrated with *The Cabala* and *Heaven's My Destination*.

Moreover, in the film version of *Our Town* the theme remained as potent as in the play despite a revised ending authorized by Wilder which permitted Emily to survive the difficult labor and return to George. Toward the close of a long, amicable series of letters with Sol Lesser, the producer of the film, Wilder assented to the revision which Lesser had quite openly explained was intended to mollify the mass audience:

> In the first place, I think Emily should live. I've always thought so. In a movie you see people so *close to* that a different relation is established. In the theatre they are halfway abstractions in an allegory; in the movie they are very concrete. So, insofar as the play is a generalized allegory, she dies—we die—they die; insofar as it's a

[7] Wilder, introduction to Gertrude Stein, *Narration* (Chicago: University of Chicago Press, 1935), p. vii.

> concrete happening it's not important that she die; it's even disproportionately cruel that she die.
>
> Let her live. The idea will have been imparted anyway.[8]

The letter should quiet those of Wilder's critics who have charged him with an attempt to exact a toll of tears from his public with this work. *Our Town* is profoundly moving, with or without the death of Emily, but it does not deal sentimentally with the passions. It treats the anxieties of humanity with such calm and precision that to comment at all upon its emotional force is to risk exaggeration. A confrontation of the play results, not in a feast of sentiment, but, on the contrary, in a painful shock to the cherished notion that the best of life is still ahead.

On December 28, 1938, less than two months after the closing of *Our Town*, occurred the opening of Wilder's second Broadway play, a farce titled *The Merchant of Yonkers*. Although the play was a failure on this showing, it came into its own as a critical and popular success in 1954 with a new title: *The Matchmaker*. The title, which shifts the emphasis from one major character to another, is Wilder's most significant revision; for the rest, apart from adding a new speech at the close to point up the theme, he merely tinkered with a few passages of dialogue. *The Matchmaker*, then, cannot be considered a new play. In a chronological study of Wilder's career, it must follow *Our Town*.

Wilder wrote *The Merchant of Yonkers* as he had translated *A Doll's House*, with Ruth Gordon in mind for the lead. To the bad fortune of the production, however, a combination of circumstances kept her from accepting the part. She could not act the role designed for her because

Jed Harris, the only director with whom she was then willing to work, was not offered the play. Wilder was still on good terms with Harris, but as much as he hoped to star Miss Gordon, he was determined that the play be staged by Max Reinhardt, whom he had admired since adolescence and had at last met in Salzburg in 1931.[9] The script was a new version of a nineteenth-century Austrian play, Johann Nestroy's *Einen Jux will er sich Machen*, which in turn had been based on an English comedy, John Oxenford's *A Well Spent Day*. Although Wilder moved the action across the Atlantic to Yonkers and New York City, his play by virtue of its Viennese origin seemed appropriate for Reinhardt's talents. This meant that a new producer as well as new leading lady had to be found, inasmuch as Harris would not produce a work which he could not direct. Herman Shumlin, a producer distinguished for his discovery of Lillian Hellman, presented the play, and Jane Cowl took the starring role.

The combination of Shumlin, Reinhardt, and Cowl was scarcely a second-rate team, but the results of their work were not such as the play required. After twenty-eight performances, the production closed down. The fault was primarily Reinhardt's; the years of staging pageants at Salzburg had given him too heavy a hand for Wilder's rapid farce. That Wilder hoped to spare the director's reputation is clear from the dedication of the printed play, which reads "To Max Reinhardt with deep admiration and indebtedness." Alexander Woollcott, however, writing to Robert Hutchins during the Boston previews, gives a hint of Wilder's true feelings: "the evening became filled with the task of helping the sorely beset Wilder get tight in the Copley-Plaza. The new Academician ... is having his troubles with the Boston try-out of his new play, a fine old-style farce rendered depressing to my

[9] Isabel Wilder.

notion by a humorless performance."[10] Sixteen years later, it seemed quite another work when at last Ruth Gordon took her part and under the direction of Tyrone Guthrie, whose sense of pace is his most valuable gift to the theater, played it brilliantly. With this production, which arrived in New York on December 5, 1955, after successful runs at the Edinburgh Festival and the West End of London, the play became one of Wilder's most popular works.

Yet *The Matchmaker*, unlike *Our Town*, cannot be called an international masterpiece. Its limitations are inherent in its form. Farce, though often ingratiating, is a slight theatrical genre, never exercising the audience's emotions or intellectual powers to the full. Wilder's recent claim that he had designed the work as a parody of the stock-company pieces of his boyhood is substantiated by the action, which retains something of the preposterousness of the rough-hewn comedies of the turn of the century.[11] But quaintness, no matter how comic, does not in itself confer value. In an earlier comment written as a promotional piece for the 1938 production, he defended the play in another way:

> Farce would seem to be intended for child-like minds still touched with grossness; but the history of the theatre shows us that the opposite is true. Farce has always flourished in ages of refinement and great cultural activity.
>
> And the reason lies where one would least expect it; farce is based on logic and objectivity.[12]

So much is true, but in its very logicality lies the weakness of farce. The pursuits and evasions which constitute a

[10] Woollcott to Hutchins, Dec. 19, 1938, in Woollcott, *Letters*, ed. Beatrice Kaufman and Joseph Hennessey (New York: Viking Press, 1944), p. 215.

[11] Wilder, *Three Plays* (New York: Harper & Brothers, 1957), p. xiii.

[12] Wilder, "Noting the Nature of Farce," New York *Times*, Jan. 8, 1939, Sec. IX, p. 1.

farcical plot are based on what appear to be sound reasons; the pursuer's reason for giving chase and his quarry's
reason for running or taking cover are understandable
insofar as the first wishes to avenge a slight on the
second, who in turn wishes to avoid him. If the threat
to the safety of both remains small, the wildness of the chase
and the repetition of motions and gestures will bring on
laughter, and all will go well for the author and his audience. But tragedy and comedy, the great theatrical modes,
are *il*logical, for it makes no sense that admirable men
should come to grief, as they do in tragedy, or that the
obviously absurd human race should somehow continue
its course through history, as it does in comedy, and therein
rests their power to stir the mind and feelings. *The Matchmaker*, on the other hand, makes only the faintest effort
to engage the sensibility of the audience. Nevertheless, it
takes on a kind of fascination, if only as a new departure
in technique for Wilder in his lifelong devotion to the theme
of acceptance.

An abrupt shift away from the presentational method of
Our Town would no doubt have been necessary for Wilder
at this point, regardless of his intention of tailoring a
work for the talents of Reinhardt and Ruth Gordon.
Insofar as he sustained a method in many ways quite new
for him through the four acts of the farce, his effort
deserves its late triumph. Deliberately creating two-
dimensional characters for the helter-skelter action, he
placed them in a colorful dream world which no more
resembles the cities of Yonkers and New York than a
child's dream of a gumdrop forest resembles wild nature.
The time is the 1880's, a period now distant enough to
render plausible, or at least comfortable, the never-never
quality of the scenes and people. Yonkers in the play is a
dour community inhabited by the misanthropic merchant
Horace Vandergelder, his lovesick niece Ermengarde,

and his two underpaid clerks Cornelius Hackl and Barnaby Tucker. New York is a pretty but distant place to which the clerks one day sneak off in search, for the first time in their lives, of adventure. Since Vandergelder goes there too, it is inevitable that their paths cross his and that their adventure is chiefly the problem of hiding from him. By the time the final curtain rings down, Vandergelder, Ermengarde, and the clerks alike have had adventures with banging doors, crashing screens, expensive dinners, and disguises. The events follow logically upon one another, but we recognize the improbability of the overall scheme of action as from one moment to the next Wilder finds ways of diverting thought from the ordinary daily life he had so carefully described in the tragedy of George Gibbs and Emily Webb.

The theme, however, is the same. "My play," Wilder wrote in 1957, "is about the aspirations of the young (and not only of the young) for a fuller, freer participation in life." [13] To sustain the sentimentality of the action as well as to point up this moral comes a simply worded but similar justification of the play at the conclusion, spoken by "the youngest person here," Barnaby Tucker:

> Oh, I think it's about . . . I think it's about adventure. The test of an adventure is that when you're in the middle of it, you say to yourself, "Oh, now I've got myself into an awful mess; I wish I were sitting quietly at home." And the sign that something's wrong with you is when you sit quietly at home wishing you are out having lots of adventure. (p. 401) [14]

Of the entire cast, the character who most effectively represents this adventurous spirit is the matchmaker herself, Mrs. Dolly Levi, a widow who pretends to arrange a marriage between Vandergelder and a mysterious

[13] Wilder, *Three Plays*, p. xiii.

[14] Quotations of *The Matchmaker* are from *Three Plays*, its first appearance in print.

friend, only to lay her own trap for him. She is a healer of varicose veins, a hosiery saleswoman, a teacher of the guitar and mandolin, and "a woman who arranges things" (p. 277); thus Wilder sketches her personality with the broad strokes appropriate to farce. For her as for Vandergelder, money is all-important; she, however, seeks it only for comfort, not, like the merchant, for a bogus kind of power. She is, then, free in spirit, not held closely in check by ignoble ambition. From the outset it is clear that she will marry Vandergelder, despite the lengthy description she delivers, by way of a borrowing from Molière's *L'Avare*, of her friend's charm and culinary expertise. She is Wilder's addition to Nestroy's plot, and a shrewd invention, since the play depends heavily upon her for its gaiety and sense.

Keeping the world at a distance from the improbable characters of this play with the same determination that he drew it in as a backdrop for the sturdy characters of *Our Town*, Wilder employs four different interior sets to confine the action to specific locales. In nineteenth-century fashion they hold us to the present moment on the stage, allowing no hint that a cruel, passionate humanity lives just the other side of the walls. But, far from being naturalistic, the scenery is the sort that calls attention to itself. For both professional productions of the play the designers, presumably with Wilder's blessing, parodied the traditional box set by painting flat, bright, conspicuously "charming" scenes which referred to, but did not precisely mirror, the style of the period. Still another mockery of convention is the device of permitting each character to come forward and reveal his attitude toward life directly to the audience as though in conversation with an intimate acquaintance. For any variety of drama in which the audience senses a gradual personal involvement, this kind of interruption so decisively impedes the action as to be ruinous, but with *The Matchmaker* it is a successful extension of the two-dimensionality which is the author's controlling principle. The thin, distorted frame of the entire work becomes all the more evident for what it is as the characters step out of the play one by one, and the theme itself, by the same token, becomes increasingly apparent as the audience finds itself drawn away from the action to a simple expression of ideas. If the world is not to be allowed into the sets, then the characters will leave the sets briefly from time to time, enter the world and describe its values, and then return to their own comfortable milieu.

That such devices provide a certain pleasure in the viewing has been apparent to theatergoers since the revival of 1954. They are, however, interesting primarily as novel methods of expression which succeed within their intentionally narrow range. At the present moment it appears likely that *The Matchmaker* will achieve longevity as a stock and community-theater piece, a turn of events indicative of the public's growing theatrical sophistication, inasmuch as the play was designed to make fun of the standard stock material of the past. But to say so much for the play is not to praise it highly, for the stock company audience is seldom demanding. It will applaud whatever is easy or momentarily bright. Wilder has not seen fit to write stylized farce a second time; according to all present indications, he has abandoned it completely. On January 16, 1964, a musical version of the piece, broader by far than the original, opened on Broadway with great success. Titled *Hello, Dolly!*, the show starred Carol Channing; the adaptation was the work of Michael Stewart, and the words and music were supplied by Jerry Herman.

After the failure of *The Merchant of Yonkers* Wilder turned in short order to new ideas for plays. His first project of major concern was a piece to be called *The Emporium*. Now discarded, it is unlikely ever to be worked up for submission to producers, since Wilder is not in the habit of refurbishing manuscripts which do not meet his standards of self-criticism. More rewarding to him was his notion of making a play out of Joyce's *Finnegans Wake*. At the MacDowell Colony in the summer of 1940 he worked at the dramatization in earnest and continued with it through 1941, with moments set aside for two important essays which he published in the same year. Both essays reveal that his mind was catching at ideas for the form and substance of the major play in the making. The first to appear was his memorial to Joyce for *Poetry: A Magazine of Verse*. After commenting at length on *Ulysses*, he concluded with remarks on *Finnegans Wake*, still a little-explored novelty: "We cannot know yet whether hate has buried this conception [of man and civilization] under the debris of language analyzed to dust or whether love through identification with human history, through the laughter of the comic genius, and through the incomparable musicality of its style, has won its greatest triumph of all." [15]

The second, longer essay, "Some Thoughts on Playwriting," is a codification of the theory of dramatic art which Wilder had developed through the 1930's and which had manifested itself in the two long plays of the decade. As such it is valuable, but despite its length it adds little to what the plays had already shown. Stress falls, as is to be expected, upon the virtues of the unadorned stage:

> If Juliet is represented as a girl "very like Juliet" . . . moving about in a "real" house with marble staircases, rugs, lamps, and furniture, the impression is irresistibly conveyed that these events happened to this one girl, in one place, at one moment in time. When the play is

[15] Wilder, "James Joyce (1882–1941)," *Poetry: A Magazine of Verse*, LVII (March 1941), 374.

staged as Shakespeare intended it, the bareness of the
stage releases the events from the particular and the
experience of Juliet partakes of that of all girls in love, in
every time, place and language.[16]

To this Wilder adds that the drama is a collaborative
effort shared by the playwright, the actors, and the
playgoers who sit "shoulder to shoulder" as the play
unfolds. Such a conception of the theatrical experience
leads to the idea of drama as a ritual in which the members of the audience are celebrants. If they are to be
reached as a community rather than as a collection of
individuals, they must receive from the playwright
materials of broad interest which they can enjoy together,
not materials limited in appeal to the interest of only a few
persons. In this observation Wilder may have had in
mind his own work-in-progress, which was to simplify,
but not dilute or cheapen, *Finnegans Wake* for the collective
understanding of the audience.

Although Wilder completed the new play in the season
of 1941–1942, he did not immediately bring it to the
stage. His last offering to the general public before
entering the Army Air Corps was the scenario for an
Alfred Hitchcock thriller, *Shadow of a Doubt*, which was
filmed in 1942. This assignment coincided with the
arrival of Wilder's commission, and to carry it out in the
scant three weeks at his disposal he worked closely
with the director and was still talking over the details of
plot when the time came to be sworn in. The amusing
upshot was that Hitchcock accompanied him on the train
from Los Angeles to New York, taking notes for the script
all along the route.[17] The plot of this picture concerns a
homicidal psychopath who revisits his home town amid

[16] Wilder, "Some Thoughts on Playwriting," in *The Intent of the Artist*,
ed. Augusto Centeno (Princeton: Princeton University Press, 1941), p. 95.
[17] Woollcott to Sibyl, Lady Colefax, Sept. 1,1942, in Woollcott, *Letters*,
p. 355.

reports of particularly grim murders which have occurred elsewhere. Gradually, but not as suspensefully as might be hoped, it becomes evident that he himself is the murderer and that if allowed to remain at large he will continue to kill. Although Hitchcock after twenty years and twenty pictures could remark in 1963 that this film is his favorite among his own works,[18] that opinion is not likely to be shared by his fans, for *Shadow of a Doubt* moves all too smoothly toward a conclusion that is obvious from the outset. The question rises whether Hitchcock would have troubled to engage Wilder had he not intended a commercial exploitation of the writer's talent for depicting small town life in several passages of village domesticity which highlight the film.

Meanwhile Wilder had finished his play and had found a title: *The Skin of Our Teeth.* He had expected Harris to produce and direct the new work and had corresponded with him about its progress since 1940. On reading the completed script, however, Harris did not approve and could not be persuaded to take it on.[19] Left in a quandary, Wilder at last turned the play over to Michael Myerberg, a young man with no producing credits but overwhelming ambition who had importuned Wilder since the success of *Our Town* to entrust a work to him. By November 18, 1942, when the play reached Broadway, Wilder was on his way to North Africa. Although his absence created some difficulty, it did not hamper the production, for Myerberg had provided an uncommonly good company. Fredric March, Florence Eldridge, and Tallulah Bankhead (in a part originally offered to Helen Hayes[20]) were the stars, and smaller parts were given to Montgomery Clift and Florence Reed. The director was Elia

---

[18] "In Charge," *New Yorker*, XXXIX (March 30, 1963), 37.

[19] Isabel Wilder.

[20] Helen Hayes to Woollcott, July 2, 1942, in Woollcott, *Letters*, p. 346.

Kazan, whose reputation for organizing brilliantly intense productions was then beginning to expand rapidly within the profession. With the play in such hands, the absent author had little to worry about. It was not until the play was settled into its run that a problem rose from it to trouble him.

Much the most complex of Wilder's plays, *The Skin of Our Teeth* presented a distinct risk on Broadway despite its merit. The play rests not only upon Joyce, but upon German expressionism, vaudeville, burlesque, and Wilder's own one-acts—a combination of forces transfusing both structure and theme. It also nods at the smug domestic dramas of the late nineteenth and early twentieth centuries and mocks their limited vision as controlled by the box set. As a wartime play written, Wilder has since said, "under strong emotion," [21] it was calculated to encourage the troubled public of 1942, but its theme is broad enough to transcend the concerns of the time and to appeal to the relatively small audience for serious plays in any year. The title itself announces the theme, which is that no matter how hard pressed or frightened, the human race has power to survive its great adventure in a world where physical nature and its own internal conflicts pose endless threats. Beneath this is the idea which forms the core of all Wilder's major works. As the action proceeds it becomes clear that the playwright holds man to be worth preserving for all his absurdity, and holds also that man's lot is worth the effort it costs him to sustain life, however great his misfortunes. For the purposes of this play, Wilder's vision of life is comic, and the action which supports the theme develops the comic possibilities of its disparate sources.

As he had done with *Our Town*, Wilder designed a presentational method which would permit the audience

[21] Wilder, *Three Plays*, p. xiii.

to be drawn toward the characters as individuals with private problems while recognizing that they also function in a broader sphere as the representatives of the entire race. This, however, is only part of a quite elaborate scheme. There is a deliberately old-fashioned, expressionistic vaudeville quality in much of the action which is reminiscent of John Howard Lawson's *Processional* of 1925 and similar plays by Lawson, Michael Gold, and John Dos Passos for the New Playwrights' Theatre of the late 1920's: plays which combine elements of the subliterary stage with the abstract characters of the contemporary expressionistic drama of Europe. It is this vaudevillesque aspect of *The Skin of Our Teeth* which led many reviewers to assert that Wilder had written his play under the influence of Ole Olsen and Chick Johnson's *Hellzapoppin*, a long-running extravaganza contrived from bits of burlesque and revue material, when in fact he had drawn nothing from it at all.[22] On the other hand, George and Maggie Antrobus and their servant Sabina occasionally take part in low-comedy clowning of the vaudeville and Keystone Cops variety at the same time that they represent Adam, Eve, and Lillith and, as the name Antrobus indicates, All Mankind. Yet, because they stand for the entire race, they must have genuine human qualities as well. To stress the essentially human, Wilder frequently lets them drop their stage roles and appear as actors who have been engaged to appear in a play titled *The Skin of Our Teeth*. The development of characters on so many planes at once requires skill in balancing and adjusting dialogue in such a way as to avoid awkwardness in the transition from one level of personality to another. Present always is the danger of baffling the audience where the intention is to instruct. Wilder's success is evident in the intensity of feeling generated by the characters, which at the

[22] Isabel Wilder.

appropriate moments reaches the heights of *Our Town* without jarring against the comic elements. In observing that the audience sees double while watching the action,[23] Wilder underestimated his achievement; the keenest members of the audience will see not merely two sorts of personality in each character, but three, four, or even five as the play unfolds.

Thus it is apparent that George Antrobus is Adam, since his family is the race itself. But he also is a burlesque comedian who greets his family with epithets bordering on the obscene, and in addition he is a go-getting American businessman, rejoicing in his invention of the wheel and the alphabet, having the time of his life at a convention (of mammals) in Atlantic City, planning impatiently to rebuild his home and his community after nature and warfare have demolished them. On the other hand, and more importantly, his inventions, his pride in the scholarly attainments, such as they are, of his children, and his overriding wish to preserve human knowledge and dignity in the face of disaster establish him as a figure representing the intellectual side of man's nature. Maggie, his wife, is Eve, the eternal homemaker and mother, cherishing even her wicked son Henry (who was called Cain before he killed his brother), looking after the well-being of the race, discovering that the tomato is edible. "If you want to know anything more about Mrs. Antrobus," her servant says, "just go and look at a tigress, and look hard" (p. 5). The home of the Antrobuses stands on Cedar Street in Excelsior, New Jersey, but like the Gibbs and Webb homes it stands at the same time in the center of creation, as the focal point of a struggling but venturesome race to sustain itself.

The sensual quality in mankind is presented by the servant Sabina, raped home like the Sabines and looking

[23] Wilder, *Three Plays*, p. xiii.

after man's desires, as opposed to Maggie, who looks after his needs. A new hat, a dish of ice cream, and a ticket to the movies are all that she requires for happiness, as Maggie remarks in a simplification of the sensual pleasures sought by humanity. By making her a comic figure, Wilder demonstrates his boundless tolerance of this element in human nature. She is potentially dangerous in one moment of the second act when she attempts to seduce Antrobus, but the scene passes too quickly to render her contemptible. Her anti-intellectualism is not confined to her roles as servant and temptress, but spills over into her personality as Miss Somerset, the hard-up actress who is taking the maid's part because no other is available. "I can't invent any words for this play," she says in desperation when Maggie fails to respond to the cue Sabina has fed her, "and I'm glad I can't. I hate this play and every word in it."

> As for me [she continues] I don't understand a single word of it, anyway,—all about the troubles the human race has gone through, there's a subject for you.
> Besides the author hasn't made up his silly mind as to whether we're all living back in caves or in New Jersey today, and that's the way it is all the way through.
> Oh—why can't we have plays like we used to have— *Peg o' My Heart*, and *Smilin' Thru*, and *The Bat*, good entertainment with a message you can take home with you?
> I took this hateful job because I had to. For two years I've sat up in my room living on a sandwich and a cup of tea a day, waiting for better times in the theater. And look at me now: I—I who've played *Rain* and the *Barretts of Wimpole Street* and *First Lady*—God in Heaven! (p. 7)

That she interrupts the action to make this complaint is in keeping with her part, inasmuch as she moves the play in the direction of comedy and renders cherishable, as an aspect of humanity, the low-brow attitude which allows no time for presumably serious drama. If the plays she mentions have messages, so of course has *The Skin of Our Teeth*, and her deliberate stopping of the action underscores them.

Another of Sabina's functions is the enhancement of the mockery of domestic drama which enters the play in the first and last acts. As the curtain rises at the start, she is present with duster in hand, like the servant in a nineteenth-century play of middle-class household intrigue, to let the audience in on the manners and means of her employers. And as she cleans the room, the flats which form its walls flap, buckle, and fly out of sight in a merry parody of the box set, letting in a glimpse of the outside world. Typical of such a part is her fear that a dire accident has befallen her master, who has not yet come home across the Hudson River. Within moments, however, he makes his appearance, and the greater dimensions of the family as Adam and Eve and their household become evident.

With the interactions of these three characters and Henry, who as Cain represents the opposing self, Wilder spreads out his view of the human condition. As the various elements of the personality are frequently at war with one another within each human being, so do these characters quarrel and complain, only to discover that they cannot exist separately. To make the whole man, thought, love, and lust play parts, and troublesome as it is, the self-destructive impulse is always present. Wilder's thought is deistic, combining a belief that God made the world and left the running of it to man with a belief that human activity is psychologically determined. The play abounds in Biblical allusions and includes a re-enactment of Noah's flood, yet at no point makes the suggestion that the race has survived its catastrophes through divine intervention. It is only by chance and the playwright's careful calculation that a ship is present to save the Antrobuses from the flood, and that two of each kind of animal are also on hand, though the action which precedes the embarkation makes obvious references to the deadly sins.

Again as with *Our Town*, Wilder stresses those traits of personality which are especially appealing, thus cajoling us into accepting the characters as representatives of ourselves. Most serviceable for this purpose are the interruptions of the action, such as Sabina's quoted above. In the last act, which occurs after the conclusion of a horrendous war, Wilder finds two such opportunities. The first is a pause brought on by the sudden illness of actors engaged to play Spinoza, Plato, Aristotle, and the author of Genesis. They were to cross the stage at the end of the play, each bearing a sign for one of the hours of the night—"a poetic effect," as the company's stage manager calls it (p. 108), borrowed from *Pullman Car Hiawatha*. Since no other actors are available, the parts must be taken by the wardrobe mistress, a maid, the captain of the ushers, and Antrobus's dresser, all of whom are glad to serve. With this device Wilder implies that the writing of the great philosophers takes effect upon the members of the race even without their awareness of it. He assigns the Negro maid the task of articulating the idea, hinting all the while that a sense of racial inferiority slows down her words and renders them tentative or apologetic:

> Excuse me, I think it means—excuse me, Mr. Fitzpatrick ... Mr. Fitzpatrick, you let my father come to a rehearsal; and my father's a Baptist minister, and he said that the author meant that—just like the hours and stars go by over our heads at night, in the same way the ideas and thoughts of the great men are in the air

around us all the time and they're working on us, even when we don't know it. (pp. 108–109)

The speech not only serves to express a concept of the intellectual life, but serves also, through its halting diction, to make an oblique plea for tolerance by warming us to the girl who speaks it.

Later, when the actor playing Henry comes close to strangling the actor playing his father, comes another passage pulsing with Wilder's humanitarian instinct. Here the younger actor attempts to show that his part in the play as the wartime enemy has elicited a harrowing response from his own, not his stage-character's, personality:

> HENRY: Nobody can say *must* to me. All my life everybody's been crossing me,—everybody, everything, all of you. I'm going to be free, even if I have to kill half the world for it. Right now, too. Let me get my hands on his throat. I'll show him. (*He advances toward* ANTROBUS. *Suddenly,* SABINA *jumps between them and calls out in her own person:*)
>
> SABINA: Stop! Stop! Don't play this scene. You know what happened last night. Stop the play. (*The men fall back, panting.* HENRY *covers his face with his hands.*) Last night you almost strangled him. You became a regular savage. Stop it!
>
> HENRY: It's true. I'm sorry. I don't know what comes over me. I have nothing against him personally. I respect him very much . . . I . . . I admire him. But something comes over me. It's like I become fifteen years old again. I . . . I . . . listen: my own father used to whip me and lock me up every Saturday night. I never had enough to eat. He never let me have enough money to buy decent clothes. I was ashamed to go downtown. I never could go to the dances. My father and my uncle put rules in the way of everything I wanted to do. They tried to prevent my living at all.—I'm sorry. I'm sorry.

MRS. ANTROBUS (*Quickly*): No, go on. Finish what you were saying. Say it all.

HENRY: In this scene it's as though I were back in High School again. It's like I had some big emptiness inside me, —the emptiness of being hated and blocked at every turn. And the emptiness fills up with the one thought that you have to strike and fight and kill. Listen, it's as though you have to kill somebody else so as not to end up killing yourself. (pp. 130–131)

Henry is getting at the basis of man's antisocial drives, but at the same time that he reveals the seriousness of the matter he offers through his familiar, boyish imagery a plea for sympathetic understanding. At such moments of the play intellectual stimulus and emotional appeal are in precise balance.

These scenes occur shortly before the conclusion of action that spans the ages from the descent of the glaciers over North America to the end of the most grotesque war in history—presumably Wilder's image of the Second World War. Of the calamities which nearly put an end to the Antrobus family, each has a different cause. The great wall of ice which brings the coldest day of the year in the middle of August is malevolent nature, with which man must do battle constantly. The family conquers it with the warmth provided by coffee, group-singing, and a fire made of beds, tables, and the seats in the theater even as the ice pushes at the walls of their house in Excelsior. In other words, common sense and heartiness are suffi-cient for overcoming disasters in the natural world. The overwhelming flood of the second act is described as a storm, but is not altogether a natural phenomenon; apparently it is also a form of retributive justice handed down by an unnamed power. Wilder's unwillingness to identify the power as God obscures his message for part of the act, but ultimately he makes it clear that man is about to be punished for his sinfulness. All the family are sinners. We see Henry in ungovernable wrath picking a fight with a Negro and thus, it would seem, initiating race hatred. Mrs. Antrobus, filled with pride that her husband is the presiding officer at the convention of mammals, insults the man who ran against him for the position. Antrobus's sin is lust; he has succumbed to the effort of Sabina, now a beauty-contest winner named Miss Fairweather, to seduce him in a beach cabana. When the storm warnings have reached their peak, the Antrobuses and Sabina, who have recovered from their wickedness, board a ship which happens to be waiting off shore and take with them the two delegates to the convention of every species of animal.

The last act, which carries the play into the present, is a stronger expression of ideas. It begins, not with the outbreak of war, but, for the happy conclusion necessary for comedy and the furtherance of the theme of survival, with the coming of peace. The enemy posited in this act is not nature or original sin in any of its specific forms, but the self-destructive instinct within the human spirit, as represented by Henry—the deep-rooted, malign force that can measure its own growth only by killing. To contend successfully with this enemy is the gravest problem of all. Mankind can at best forge an uneasy truce with it by closely analyzing the phenomena which created it, as the actor taking the part of Henry attempts to do. When Henry is pacified for the time being by the sensual Sabina, it is possible to go on with the business of living, as though nothing worse could possibly happen. But Wilder is not so unastute as to wish to urge upon the audience the notion that evil is absolutely to be abolished with the end of the war, for the accumulated evidence of the millions of years of human life gives such a notion the lie. The ending, then, is only tentative. After a blackout the lights come up on Sabina in the Excelsior living room, her feather duster in her hand—precisely her stance at the beginning of the play.

At first thought it is astonishing that a play so full of stops, starts, tricks, and dodges should lay a strong grip upon the emotions. It is saved from archness by Wilder's humanity, which expresses itself in this play as in all the others through ordinary speech, though it does so in the midst of many-layered, allusive dialogue and commensurately complex action. In this respect the play bears a resemblance to the most stageworthy of the works of Bertolt Brecht, which despite the songs, lantern slides, and printed messages intended to hold the audience at a distance, are capable of arousing great feeling. Especially in the confrontations of the members of the Antrobus family with one another is the simplicity of speech effective. Families are families, even when the members are figures in an allegory, as Wilder had previously demonstrated in *Our Town*. Wilder's only defensive reply to his critics to date on any score has come as a response to complaints that *The Skin of Our Teeth* is "a bookish fantasia about history, full of rather bloodless schoolmasterish jokes." [24] This he believes is not its usual effect, and for substantiation he cites productions in postwar Germany at which he witnessed gratifyingly warm reactions in the audience. It is not, however, a foolproof play. The production demands are very heavy, not only in comparison to *Our Town* but to the majority of twentieth-century plays, both as to stage equipment and acting skill. This limitation became apparent in the American production of 1955, when the play dwindled into dullness as a result of the inept performances of George Abbott as Mr. Antrobus and Mary Martin as Sabina. But, production difficulties notwithstanding, as the world spins

[24] *Ibid.*, p. xiii.

from crisis to crisis, the play continues to live. It is certain to remain in the repertory of the intellectual theater. In 1964 plans were announced for a musical version, with Betty Comden and Adolph Green as librettists and Leonard Bernstein as composer.

The strongest complaints against *The Skin of Our Teeth* have risen, not in discussions of its theatrical viability, but in remarks on its sources. In December 1942 a thunderous controversy was initiated with two articles written for the *Saturday Review of Literature* by Henry Morton Robinson and Joseph Campbell, the young scholars then at work on the book ultimately to be published as *A Skeleton Key to Finnegans Wake*.[25] Unable to discriminate between the legitimate assimilation of a source and downright theft, they accused Wilder of plagiarism and of the debasement of Joyce's work. Although they proceeded beyond reason in their charges, they were correct enough in pointing to the similarity of the play to the novel. It is evident in the structure itself, which like that of the novel is circular, repeating the lines of the opening at the close. It is evident also in the resemblance between the Antrobuses and the Earwickers of the *Wake*, and in the procedure of describing all history through the family's activity, the past mixed in with the present and the banal mixed in with the profound. One serious result of the controversy was the refusal of the members of the New York Drama Critics Circle to present their annual award to Wilder, despite the obvious superiority of his play to all others of the season. Partial compensation for this injustice came soon afterward with the bestowal of the Pulitzer Prize.

Although the charges of plagiarism still come up in

[25] See Robinson and Campbell, "The Skin of Whose Teeth?" Pts. I and II, *Saturday Review of Literature*, XXV (Dec. 19, 1942), 3–4; XXVI (Feb. 13, 1943), 16, 18–19.

introductions to the play for text anthologies and were renewed by Robinson as late as March 1957 in an article for *Esquire*, they are now largely, and properly, ignored. Equally unsound, and now dropped, is the charge that the play cheapens the novel. To reach the general audience, as opposed to the coterie audience of the academic theater, Wilder found it necessary to broaden the substance of the book in order to clarify it. Professorial adaptations of passages of the novel have come along in the years since, but they cannot survive outside the academic theater and even there make no great impact.[26] Remaining silent through the heat of the controversy, Wilder appeared to be taking for granted that his public would recognize honest borrowing for what it was. At last in the preface to *Three Plays*, published in October 1957, he acknowledged his source: "The play is deeply indebted to James Joyce's *Finnegans Wake*. I should be very happy if, in the future, some author should feel similarly indebted to any work of mine. Literature has always more resembled a torch race than a furious dispute among heirs" (p. xiv). Should Wilder make a practice of studying the writers of the so-called Theater of the Absurd, who rely on slapstick, allegory, and seeming non-sequiturs for their reports on the meaning of existence, he would see the debts mounting.

[26] The present writer recalls a performance of Leon Katz's *Finnegans Wake* (unpub.) at Vassar College, Dec. 1951 (on Anna Livia Plurabelle); also, see Mary Manning, *Passages from Finnegans Wake* (Cambridge, Mass.: Harvard University Press, 1957). On the other hand, Jean Erdman's *The Coach with the Six Insides*, an adaptation of the novel with dance, pantomime, and song, played well when presented off Broadway in the 1962-1963 season.

VI. Postwar Writing

WILDER'S FIRST SUBSTANTIAL postwar work, *The Ides of March*, did not appear until January 1948, two and a half years after his separation from the service. Although an account, whether factual or in the guise of creative literature, of the war as he had witnessed it might have found a cordial public, he turned, for the first time since *The Cabala*, to antiquity and produced "a fantasia on certain persons and events of the last days of the Roman republic" (p. vii). The beauty of the Italian *campagna*, in which he had enjoyed walks during the war, had stimulated him to return in fiction to Rome.[1] The recent deaths of the twentieth-century dictators may have prompted him to write of Julius Caesar,[2] with whose death the novel ends, but his portrait of Caesar bears no resemblance to any other dictator of either the remote or the more recent past. Nor can the events described in the book be construed as projections of the European disasters which

---

[1] See Wilder's comments in Brooks Atkinson, introduction to *The Ides of March* (New York: Harper & Brothers, 1950), p.xii (not included in the first edition of 1948); Isabel Wilder.

[2] Atkinson, *loc. cit.*

he had seen at close range during the war. A new expression of an old theme, the novel recommends intense participation in life according to a conscience wise by nature and training—Caesar's conscience—and regardless of personal peril.

The most intricately constructed of Wilder's novels, *The Ides of March* is comparable to a set of bowls placed one within another. It is divided into four sections, the first covering only one month, with each of the others embracing a longer time span than that preceding it. Thus certain scenes are repeated frequently, and always from a new viewpoint. On breaking his vow of the mid-1930's to write no more novels, Wilder was at pains to develop methods insuring that in its structure this work would bear no resemblance to his earlier fiction. To avoid the presence of the all-knowing author, that seeming necessity of fiction, he presents the entire plot in a documentary style, or, rather, a pseudo-documentary style, since the letters, state papers, and diaries which make up the text are of his own invention. Only Suetonius's description of the assassination and some poems by Catullus are authentic. Throughout the novel he plays freely with Roman history, altering the records to suit his needs. Many of the participants in the action had died long before the few months which it covers; the most important among them are Catullus, Clodius Pulcher, and Caesar's aunt Julia Marcia. Moreover, a number of the crucial events had occurred well in the past. It is through the deliberate manipulation of history that *The Ides of March* becomes the fantasia Wilder has labeled it, and through the same process also that the theme emerges.

Aware that many of his readers would recognize the distortions of truth in his narrative for what they are, Wilder prepared in advance for their criticism. His prefatory comments include a list of all the anachronisms.

He has subsequently extended these remarks to explain his method in part, as though acknowledging that the book is a kind of stunt and exhibiting worry over his ability to bring it off. He claims that by avoiding dialogue, which appears only as reported conversation in the mock-diaries, he has given the novel something of the quality of drama. Without the "he said" and "she said" customary to narrative technique, it is possible to keep the book in the present, even though its material is historical. All the documents are present-tense items and are therefore seemingly fresh from their writers' hands. Being of the opinion that in our age of psychoanalysis it is absurd for a writer untrained in that science to pretend to total knowledge of the minds of others, he hoped also by this method to free himself of the burden of revealing the activity in the characters' minds of which they themselves were not conscious.[3] In this attempt he could not be utterly successful, to be sure, for the process of selecting attitudes to be reflected in the documents is only the novelist's traditional omniscience in new form. Yet, by virtue of its novelty the method is effective in drawing the reader along.

The disregard of strict chronology is another deterrent to the process of dissociation which Wilder had hoped to carry out. Both in the design of the ever-expanding coverage of the four sections and in the inclusion in 45 and 44 B.C. of much earlier events his own hand can clearly be seen at work, not merely to shape an intrigue, but to shape it for the expression of a theme. Here lies our chief clue to the meaning of the novel, for the last months of Caesar's life exactly as he lived them would provide material enough for fiction without the

[3] Wilder, statement in *The World's Best*, ed. Whit Burnett (New York: Dial Press, 1950), pp. 104–105; see also Glenway Wescott, *Images of Truth* (New York: Harper & Row, 1962), pp. 267–269.

inclusion of incidents presented out of historical context. Each of the four divisions shows Caesar in a light of its own as he meditates on religion, power, love, and destiny, his thoughts in part determined by the activities of the highest-placed personages of Rome. In essence, his query centers on the problem of transcending the demands of his position—put another way, freeing himself from his obligation to history—in order to achieve contentment in life. "You talk of the past," he writes to his beloved aunt. "I do not let my thoughts dwell on it for long. All of it, all of it, seems of a beauty that I shall not see again. . . . Can other men weave past joy into their thoughts in the present and their plans for the future? Perhaps only the poets can; they alone use all of themselves in every moment of their work" (p. 20). This echo of *Our Town* is Wilder's theme, obliquely expressed. It is so distinctly identifiable with his work as a whole that once it is uttered no elaboration of technique could remove our awareness of his presence behind the action. The manipulation of time, far from separating him from the book, only draws him more intimately into it as he plots the moves whereby he will impress the theme upon us.

Book One, which concentrates on events of September 45 B.C., gives the essence of Caesar's personality and introduces the persons closest to him, with the exception of Cleopatra, who enters the novel in the next book. Under the dictatorship of Caesar, Rome has altered and is continuing to alter. Behind many of the reforms which he constantly institutes lies the purpose of bringing back the dignity and morality which his aunt and other elderly ladies refer to as "old Rome." Thus he has put through a series of sumptuary regulations and has attempted to strengthen and dignify the religious ceremonies of the state. Other governmental actions, some mentioned in Book One and some not until later, are the establishment of public libraries, the shifting of the course of the Tiber, and revisions of the penal code, all of which point toward the greatness of the Empire to come. Yet these moves do not satisfy him, for he is plagued with questions about the existence of the gods and ready to abandon state religion altogether for the moral strengthening of the people if only he can convince himself that man is the center of the universe. "I must be certain," he writes to his friend Lucius Mamilius Turrinus, "that in no corner of my being there lingers the recognition that there is a possibility of a mind in and behind the universe which influences our minds and shapes our actions" (p. 38). This, the central problem of his life, he cannot resolve. At the end of Book One, however, comes something like an answer. He hears a suggestion from the poet Catullus, delivered in an impromptu version of the legend of Alcestis, that it is impossible to distinguish between the spirit of the gods and the spirit of man, and at once suffers an epileptic seizure, a physical collapse which for him is always a kind of ecstasy.

In Book Two Caesar concerns himself primarily with love. The subject is heralded by letters on the imminent arrival of Cleopatra, for whom Caesar has a passion which despite the passage of years is still colored by his awe that a woman so sensuous could be so wise. It is impossible for him to love a woman whom he cannot teach; when long ago Cleopatra accepted his advice on governing and demonstrated her ability as a ruler, she became the object of his love. Occasionally impatient with her pretensions although he himself fostered them, he nevertheless finds her to be the one woman of consummate allure since the death of Cornelia, his first wife.

Contrasted to Cleopatra in Book Two and throughout the later books are two other women caught up in erotic relationships: Clodia Pulcher, the "Lesbia" of Catullus's poems, and Cytheris, the mistress of Mark Antony. The most vividly drawn of the women in the novel, Clodia is as intelligent as Cleopatra, but, driven into hatred of humanity by a hideous event of her childhood—violation by her uncle—she uses her mind principally for the invention of schemes to madden others. She herself is the mysterious disease which causes the death of Catullus, so great a poet that in Caesar's regard he is one of the principal ornaments of the state. In her destructive frenzy, Clodia torments not only the poet, but Caesar himself, out of envy and admiration for his self-possession. In Book One she writes to him passionately for that special scrap of knowledge which makes life tolerable for him, but which she has been denied. Through her personality as much as through Caesar's, the novel offers the suggestion that the expectancy of a life to come cannot compensate for emptiness in the present moment. Both are skeptical and dissatisfied, but neither has a clear notion of what lies ahead.

Cytheris, on the other hand, is content with the present. The ambition of Cleopatra and the dissatisfaction of Clodia are problems such as she has never had to endure. The greatest actress of her time, she rests secure in the comfort of her artistry, her mind free to speculate on the meaning of the activity around her. Only she, Caesar, and Julia Marcia in all of Rome are the confidants of the noble Lucius Mamilius Turrinus, the friend of Caesar from boyhood who after suffering mutilation and blinding at the hands of the Gauls secluded himself permanently in Capri. To this extraordinarily gifted man, a Roman counterpart of Wilder's friend Edward Sheldon, the three send letters and make annual journeys. That he allows Cytheris within his circle is a measure of her greatness. The actress's moment of triumph occurs at the end of Book Two, when she and the two younger women of the novel are brought together in a striking scene. To destroy Caesar's calm, Clodia plots with Mark Antony a feat of great daring: he is to attempt a seduction of Cleopatra on the night when, as a newly arrived state visitor, she gives her reception for the leaders of Rome. The two are caught by Caesar himself and are helpless to conceal from him that Antony has indeed made advances and that Cleopatra has not been altogether determined to fend them off. For Cytheris, as she tells Lucius Mamilius, this is the beginning of a new life without Antony, and although she is pained by his rejection of her as mistress, she is capable of adjusting to a stage in life when friendship replaces love: "a bell rang; a music ceased" (p. 140). Caesar, equally hurt by what has happened, presumably learns something from the experience also. Precisely what it means to him Wilder leaves uncertain, but the tone of his last, brief letter of Book Two to Cleopatra implies that he sees the process of living out a life as the process of learning to encounter dismay courageously.

Like the first book, Book Three presents Caesar's thoughts on religion and the welfare of the state, but reaches out to embrace fresh aspects of these subjects. Running through the novel like a low fever is talk of the preparations for the festival of the Good Goddess in early December, a rite reserved for the women of Rome's first families. Caesar's aunt is to preside over the ceremony, which is a secret performance lasting through a long evening. Aware for many years that the activities of the final hours are erotic, perhaps even obscene, Caesar in accordance with his principles of strengthening the state through stern morality takes up hints from Julia Marcia and the President of the College of Vestal Virgins that the ceremony should be altered to remove the objectionable matters. He does not know the details of the ritual, since it is attended by women exclusively, but he is anxious lest it or any other holy ceremony be cheapened. In this as in his resolutions with Cleopatra he is to be disappointed.

Again it is Clodia Pulcher who is the destroyer. In Book Three her machinations result in two disasters for the state: the death of Catullus and the profanation of the mysteries of the Good Goddess. "Great poetry—" says Caesar in Book One,

> poetry is indeed the principal channel by which all that most weakens man has entered the world; there he finds his facile consolations and the lies that reconcile him to ignorance and inertia; I count myself second to no man in my hatred of all poetry save the best— but great poetry, is that merely the topmost achievement of the man's powers or is that a voice from beyond man?
>
> (p. 39)

In the work of Catullus, Caesar believes, Roman literature has reached greatness, and he is concerned, consequently, for the poet's welfare. That Clodia is driving him to a collapse is clear from much evidence. Deprived of the power to love deeply, she delights in making him miserable, reserving her greatest affection for her brother Clodius, with whom she is reported to have had incestuous relations. Knowing that she once expressed passion, in her way, for Caesar, Catullus begins a campaign of chain letters against the Dictator. This plot Wilder based upon an actual drive initiated against Mussolini by the Italian poet Lauro de Bossis, who shares the dedication of the novel with Edward Sheldon.[4] Yet it would seem that Catullus, unlike de Bossis, is less the patriot than the jealous lover. Caesar, not concerned about the letters and the epigrams of disapproval which the poet spreads, fears only that Catullus will die before he can bestow upon the state the poetry of which he is capable. His fear is borne out when, suffering from the taunts of Clodia, Catullus

---

[4] For a biographical sketch of de Bossis, see Wescott, pp. 280–283.

sinks into an undiagnosed disease. Caesar is present at
the deathbed, and lest Catullus think that he has lived
to no purpose, he praises Clodia as though she were the
foremost woman of the world, when in fact he despises
her.

As Wilder points out in the prefatory remarks, Book
Four brings together all the topics on which Caesar
speculates in the first three books and presents a summation of his thought in the few months before his death.
We see him worried, as always, over the good of the state,
which for him means preserving the health of Catullus
no less effortfully than contemplating new reforms and
construction projects, and we see him wrestling still with
questions of love and religion. From the reports of his
agents he knows that Catullus is behind the chain letters
signed by a "Council of Twenty," and is aware that there
is in fact no council and no other person than the poet
himself in the movement. Yet he writes to Catullus that
he must attempt to stop his supposed confederates from
issuing the letters, presumably out of fear that he will
eventually feel pressure from the Senate to apprehend
Catullus for treason. In reply, Catullus writes the truth,
that he alone is the Council.

Caesar's feeling for Brutus is much the same as his
feeling for the poet, for he believes that Brutus is another
asset to the state, although he has gradually become aware
that the younger man is aligned with the senators now
conspiring to assassinate him. An earlier, botched attempt
to slay him he dismisses as unimportant; it was the work
of Clodius Pulcher in all probability, and perhaps the
wretched Clodia lurked somewhere behind it, though this
is unlikely. Caesar offers a praetorship to Brutus and also
writes of his hope that Brutus will be his successor.
Cassius too, though known to be a malcontent, receives
a praetorship. Setting self-interest so far aside that he

seems totally indifferent to his own safety, Caesar thus continues to work for the progress of Rome. It is not through ignorance of the gathering coalition against him that he advances the two men and treats Brutus with special affection. He moves through life in a pattern incomprehensible to most men, never blind to dangers, but never avoiding them; "for it is by taking a leap into the unknown that we know we are free" (p. 238)—free to experience the very limits of the humanly possible.

Love, entwined in Caesar's thoughts with his ideas of statecraft, enters Book Four on its opening page. The first document is a letter from Servilia to her son Brutus, urging him to take a stand with the conspirators against the Dictator. One of the number of women who in the past took part in the political life of Rome, Servilia now is merely a dismally complaining creature who is eager to be noticed. But her hostility toward Caesar feeds upon a more complicated feeling than ambition for a place in the public show. It is the feeling of the rejected lover; she cannot forget that Caesar loved her once and made her a present of an extraordinary rose-colored pearl, the biggest ever seen. In defiance of the sumptuary laws, she continues to wear it. In his treatment of the coolness between the mother and son and the affection of Caesar for Brutus, Wilder brings up the question of Brutus's unknown father. Was it Caesar himself? Though aware that no evidence exists to point firmly toward the blood relationship, he nevertheless hints at it as a possible clue to Caesar's regard for the younger man and as a device for coloring the final moments of the novel with pathos. Love has disappointed Caesar before—with Cleopatra on the night of the reception; with Pompeia, his second wife, after the profanation of the rites of the Good Goddess, in which she appears to have been involved— and it disappoints him again when Brutus dismisses the proposal to think of himself as Caesar's successor. What is left? Continual fascination with life and constant experimentation, continual speculation on religion ("the unknowable") until the last moment in the Senate and the final failure of all his effort.

Any work such as this in which the portrait of Caesar is sympathetic must convey a sense of the tragic. Caesar's death is an occasion for sorrow. Brutus, no less than any of the others, cannot see beyond the immediate present; all the conspirators have chafed under the restraints imposed upon them by Caesar's reforms and are impatient to recreate Rome in their own image. As he is revealed in *The Ides of March*, Caesar is tragic not merely because he dies before his work is finished, but because of the grandeur of the ambition in which he fails, the ambition to reconstruct Rome in soaring excellence. We cannot miss Wilder's admiration for his hero, and we must not read into the novel a comparison of Caesar with the dictators of twentieth-century Europe, despite the allusion to the attempt of de Bossis to shake Mussolini from his unmerited position. As he plots the action document by document, he carefully reshapes history to deepen the tragedy inherent in Caesar's career from the first. By means of the outrageous scheming of Clodia, the chain letters of Catullus, and Brutus's denial of loyalty, he shows Caesar's career to be a series of disappointments. Yet, unlike other Wilder protagonists whether tragic or comic, Caesar does not fail to realize the value of life while living it and does not lack the talent for enjoyment. This is an unexpected turn. The familiar theme of the need for an ever-increasing understanding of experience is there as before, but the mood is different, and we are to believe that life when lived fully may bring sorrow.

Supporting this position is the existentialist philosophy of Jean-Paul Sartre, Wilder's new acquaintance of the postwar years. Unable to abandon entirely the Christian tenets which he had held all his life, Wilder does not go so far with Sartre's philosophy as to present an atheistic Caesar, but he shows a Caesar profoundly in doubt. His Caesar wishes to forswear the gods, is appalled by the decadence evident in the popular worship of himself and the new participation in Egyptian rites, yet holds always to the belief in an ordering principle behind human life, and wishes to reform the religious ceremonies of Rome for the good of his people. Thus at the end of Book One Catullus's tale of Alcestis with its implication that the gods exist, but are inconsequential, so exhilarates him that he undergoes an attack of epilepsy. Insofar as Wilder retains a belief in divinity, as Caesar's uncertainty would show him to do, his existentialism is closer to Søren Kierkegaard's than to Sartre's. He has observed privately that of Sartre's philosophy he can accept only as much as is based upon the writing of Kierkegaard.[5] But upon this foundation of nagging belief, which is no less necessary for him than atheism is for Sartre, he has constructed the portrait of a man as tormented as the lives depicted in Sartre's own fiction and drama.

The preoccupation of the existentialists with anguish is never absent from the character of Caesar in the novel. His commitment to a course of action on behalf of the state is total, yet it leads him to constant frustration and sorrow. Like the existentialists, he knows that freedom comes only in action and that to evade a difficult obligation is to surrender oneself to the durance of shame for the dubious reward of personal security—for himself specifically, safety from the menace of the conspirators. Although his point of view becomes sufficiently clear to us through such actions as his preferential treatment of the potentially dangerous Catullus, Brutus, and Cassius, it is amplified

[5] Isabel Wilder.

by Wilder in the letters to Lucius Mamilius Turrinus. Again and again Caesar ponders the course of his life, recognizing that it is perilous, but resolute in following it to the inevitable end. "I am accustomed to being hated," he writes in Book One.

> Already in early youth I discovered that I did not require the good opinion of other men, even of the best, to confirm me in my actions. . . . I hold that we cannot be said to be aware of our minds save under responsibility and that no greater danger could befall mine than that it should reflect an effort to incur the approval of any man, be it a Brutus or a Cato. I must arrive at my decisions as though they were not subject to the comment of other men, as though no one were watching. (p. 34)

Gathering courage after the desecration of the mysteries of the Good Goddess, Caesar writes again:

> Let me then banish from my mind the childish thought that it is among my duties to find some last answer concerning the nature of life. Let me distrust all impulses within me to say at any moment that it is cruel or kind, for it is no less ignoble from a situation of misery to pronounce life evil than from one of happiness to call it good. Let me not be the dupe of well-being or content, but welcome all experience that reminds me of the myriad cries of execration and of delight that have been wrung from men in every time. (p. 232)

Thus knowing life only by living it, taking the path of most resistance, Caesar proceeds toward the fatal day in March as determined to measure life by experience as the Orestes of Sartre's *Les Mouches* or the imprisoned underground fighters of his *Morts sans sépulture*.

The reworking of classical history in terms of new philosophy is an unfamiliar procedure. Because it requires out and out distortion of factual material, it goes down hard with literalists, whereas revisions of mythical or legendary anecdotes do not. The public has long been accustomed to new versions, especially in drama, of the legends of the house of Atreus, Oedipus, and Orpheus and Eurydice as presented by Jean Cocteau, Jean Anouilh, Eugene O'Neill, André Gide, T. S. Eliot, and Sartre, not to mention dozens of less competent playwrights and poets. But with matters of fact it is quite another thing, and as a result of our concern for accurate reporting Wilder's novel has suffered under the strictures of reviewers who have not understood his intention. *The Ides of March* has not been neglected, but it has received only a grudging acclaim as a bookish curiosity, more intelligent than many modern romances based on the life of ancient Greece or Rome, but odd nevertheless. The form of the novel and the pedantic explicitness of the documents, their style borrowed from Cicero's letters,[6] their wordiness reminiscent of nineteenth-century translations, create difficulties for readers who have enjoyed the comparative forthrightness of *The Bridge of San Luis Rey*. Nevertheless, by virtue of Wilder's closeness to the life of the characters, his skill in drawing them forward and then causing them to recede as points of view shift with the writers of the documents, *The Ides* is close in merit to *Heaven's My Destination*. With the exception of George Brush, Caesar is Wilder's best-drawn character in fiction, viewed like Hamlet from all sides, constantly the topic of conversation, and fully revealed through his own words. Clodia Pulcher, Cleopatra, and Julia Marcia are nearly as well realized, each with her private attitude toward Rome. Less successful, but possibly less important, are the other men; with Catullus especially we could wish for a less sketchy presentation. But above other considerations, the novel is the most comprehensive literary exposition of the existentialist conception of life created thus far in America. It is not a primer for

[6] Atkinson, p. xii.

study in Sartre's school of thought and is not uncritical of that school, but it takes effect as a probing analysis of what is still the most firmly entrenched system of belief to be disseminated since the Second World War. The unsuccessful attempt of the actor-playwright Jerome Kilty to dramatize the novel by making dialogue of the documents proved, ironically, a confirmation of Wilder's sense of form. Using the original title, the play opened in London on August 8, 1963. Despite the presence in the cast of Sir John Gielgud as Caesar and Irene Worth as Clodia, it was a quick failure.

Wilder's writing since *The Ides of March* is best described as tentative. He has withdrawn much of it for revision and has jettisoned some completed pieces altogether, as though growing continually more cautious, with the advancement of age, over what should bear his name. The quality of the works released in print is notable, but for the most part they are short.

Of the lectures on American literature which he delivered in the academic year 1950–1951 as Charles Eliot Norton Professor at Harvard, Wilder to date has published three. Though stimulating, they hold few surprises. Together they are a development of the notions on the formation of a national style impressed upon him by Gertrude Stein. Whereas the English, according to Wilder, were inclined to create literature for a homogeneous society, the Americans of the nineteenth century wrote for a mass of oddly assorted varieties of human being. This is the essence of the talks.

The American writers and their readers as Wilder describes them were descendants of the odd, curious, difficult, or disconnected persons who left their island to explore the new continent. One manifestation of the writers' attempt to reach an audience different from the

English was the development of a new language, different from British English in its use of simple and even vulgar terms—for example, Melville's use of gerunds throughout *Moby Dick* where ordinary nouns would serve. But in Wilder's reading, the prose of the nineteenth-century Americans is exceedingly specific at the same time that it is simple. The constant naming of objects, as in Walt Whitman's catalogues, he relates to the American sense of individuality, for inasmuch as a number of Americans standing together form a group of unique beings rather than an undifferentiated mass, it must appear to the American mind that the landscape or cityscape is made up of a number of things disconnected or strangely lumped together. Writing for *everybody*, the authors mention *everything*, giving each reader something to contemplate with which he may be especially familiar. In his lecture on Emily Dickinson comes Wilder's most provocative, and most questionable, contribution to the Steinian theory: the notion that the lack of finish in her poems is a deliberate eschewal of the "work of art," and this tendency he also relates to the American sense of movement and impatience with confinement. Perfection, Wilder suggests, hems in or even vitiates an idea, whereas the work left in an unfinished state is still in flux and therefore expandable to include a broader range of thought.

In preparing these talks for publication Wilder hit upon the ingenious scheme of adding italicized paragraphs representing his thoughts before and during his delivery of them to the Harvard audience. In these paragraphs he ruminates on the lecture as a means of communication, allowing his mind to wander back to the age of summer seminars at Chautauqua, when Americans gathered together to increase their knowledge in a great range of fields—a fitting introduction to a talk in which he is to mention the American absorption with detail. He ponders also the problem of formality which the lecturer to his embarrassment must often face, and silently commends Archibald MacLeish for the brevity of his introductory remarks to the crowd. This in turn leads to thoughts on the impatience developing among Americans with such formal modes of communication as the "Dear Sirs" of our letters and the traditional language of invitations as given in etiquette books. With each unspoken thought he leads into reflections in the lectures on the classlessness of American society. Had he completed the book based on these lectures which he projected in 1952, he might well have brought off a new conception of form as notable as the major plays and *The Ides of March*—that is, a work exciting to its readers not merely as a novelty, but as a strikingly intelligent treatment of an important subject in which form mirrors idea. However, he has apparently abandoned the plan to put the series into hard covers.

From his stint as a lecturer, Wilder turned again to the theater and in 1954 made the scant revisions of *The Merchant of Yonkers* which resulted in the success of *The Matchmaker*. In the following year his new tragedy, originally titled *The Alcestiad*, but renamed *A Life in the Sun* at the suggestion of Tyrone Guthrie, was as poorly received as the farce had been praised. Neither Guthrie's direction and extensive cutting of the text nor the presence of Irene Worth in the cast could save it. The play has not yet been produced or published in America, and, since Wilder has turned to other projects, it is not likely to be introduced here in the future. A version translated into German "*aus dem Amerikanischen*" and titled *Die Alkestiade* is the only published text of the play currently available. Yet, despite his indifference toward showing the tragedy at home, Wilder has demonstrated its importance to him by preparing a second version for an operatic setting by Louise Talma. It is not a work to be dismissed summarily.

We would be more correct to say that Wilder has

prepared three treatments of the Alcestis story, of which the play and the opera are the second and third. The first makes up the concluding section of Book One of *The Ides of March*, in the narrative of Catullus. Since the documentary form of the novel does not permit Wilder to interpret Caesar's reaction directly, we are left to judge it for ourselves and are likely to conclude, as noted above, that the convulsion occurs as a result of Caesar's immense joy in the poet's curious idea of divinity. As Catullus tells the legend, it begins, well before the familiar version of Euripides, with the distress of Alcestis that she must give over her ambition to become a priestess of Apollo at Delphi in favor of marriage with Admetus, King of Thessaly. She has no choice in view of her father's promise of her hand to the king, and what is more, she has not yet received the call from Apollo which could convince her to go to Delphi despite the engagement. Even at Thessaly before the ceremony she waits for a sign and postpones the marriage in the hope that it will come. She asks Admetus for permission to travel to Delphi as a servant, if not as a priestess, when startling news comes that Teresias, the priest of the oracle, is now at the palace. He has a message for her that Apollo will spend a year on earth and is present as one of five herdsmen standing outside the palace gate. When Alcestis approaches these men late in the evening to beg a word from Apollo, she receives an answer from one of them that all five have certain attributes of Apollo, but that none of them truly resembles a god in deportment. At this moment Caesar collapses—that is, at the moment when he hears a suggestion that the gods exist, but are not wholly distinguishable from men, or, put in another way, that what is human may embrace elements of the divine.

All this Wilder retains in the first act of the play, proceeding on to the marriage and following with two more acts and a satyr play to offer a brief modern equivalent of a day's fare in the Theater of Dionysus. The Christian existentialism of *The Ides of March* is present again in this work which stems from it. Alcestis is an existentialist heroine, willing to give her life to save her husband when word comes from Delphi that a wound he has received will kill him unless another desires to die in his place, since to do so clearly appears to be her responsibility. It is not that she harbors a death wish, but that she sees the road to death as a road leading on to life. In other words, death represents for her the fulfillment of a duty which enables her truly to live. But she is also a pre-Christian saint whose act of martyrdom converts the sinner Hercules, the hero given to drink and heretofore unwilling to take on the ultimate labor of wrestling with death. Observing her bravery, he is so emboldened that he descends to the underworld and leads Alcestis back to the living.

In the final act, set twenty years later, the saintliness of Alcestis remains in evidence to bring the play to a triumphant close. Admetus is killed by a usurper, the new King Agis, and Alcestis becomes a slave. But when her one surviving son comes back from exile to free her and overthrow Agis, she encourages him to work with the king to free the land of the plague under which it now suffers. From the god Apollo she then hears that she herself, the true believer, is the very sign of the existence of the gods that for many years she sought. With this the plague lifts, and Agis flees. Apollo beckons to Alcestis to join him, and, though feeble and almost blind, she answers the summons. Thus at the close as Alcestis is united with the god, Wilder demonstrates that what is mortal is potentially divine. In believing through the years of unhappiness and selflessness that the god exists, she herself has given meaning to life and has made the discovery, familiar to Wilder's characters, that all events in human existence, the bad with the good, have transcendent value.

Titled *The Drunken Sisters*, the satyr play adds to the legend an account of the measures taken by Apollo to win the release of Admetus from death. In disguise, the god makes a journey to the three Fates, gives them enough wine to make them drunk, and through a ruse secures the life of the king, all as planned, but cannot prevent their demanding another life in exchange, and cannot make them consent to take a mere slave as the substitute. They will not "murder" another person by taking his life before his thread runs out, but if a human being with the will to die appears, they will accept his sacrifice. In this sketch Wilder sustains the existentialist theme by asserting that free will has sway over "fate"—that is, over what may seem to be an unalterable course of events.

Although Wilder's philosophy is of more than passing interest as a variant of the existentialist metaphysic, and especially so in view of the ease with which he fuses it to his notions of the process of daily living, he did not find in *The Alcestiad* the means to present it dramatically. At no moment does the play muster the force of *The Ides of March*, in which the identical position supports clearly wrought scenes, fascinating not only as philosophical argument but as dramatic intrigue. Too little happens in his version of the legend to give it the stage life it needs. By coincidence, this was the second occasion on which Irene Worth appeared at the Edinburgh Festival in an adaptation of the *Alcestis* of Euripides; in 1949 she had acted in T. S. Eliot's *The Cocktail Party*. But neither she nor Guthrie was able to breathe into Wilder's work the excitement Eliot had provided.

The task which Wilder next set himself, cycles of one-act plays on the seven deadly sins and the seven ages of man, promises when finished to be the great work of his long career. At present he has set it aside, but it is to be hoped that he will soon return to it. It is to be a summation of the philosophy expounded in all his antecedent work, but deepened and broadened by the insights of the last years. To provide for fourteen plays on which he can rest secure in the knowledge that they will present cogently the ideas on which he has spent a lifetime is no small matter. It necessitates ruthless self-criticism and the setting aside of scripts which in the final proof of playing do not stand up. *Berniece*, representing the sin of pride, he has tentatively discarded, and it remains to be seen whether *The Drunken Sisters*, which was intended to represent the sin of gluttony, will remain in the cycle. "Some are on the stove, some are in the oven, and some are in the wastebasket," he has declared. "There are no first drafts in my life. An incinerator is a writer's best friend." [7]

In Theodore Mann and Jose Quintero of the Circle in the Square, Wilder found producers willing to commit themselves to the staging of the miniature dramas as they came from his desk. The partnership of the two producers has since dissolved, but the theater still stands, with Mann in charge and new directors summoned to replace Quintero. It was not through chance or prolonged search that Wilder settled on this Bleecker Street house, but through the conviction that an arena stage is the only appropriate structure for the fourteen plays and that of all such theaters, this is the most intelligently managed. Strictly speaking, the Circle in the Square is not an arena, but a structure permitting the audience to sit on three sides only, thus resembling the general plan of the theaters of Periclean Athens and Renaissance England, when no seats were stretched out in rows before the players

[7] Arthur Gelb, "Thornton Wilder, 63, Sums Up Life and Art in New Play Cycle," New York *Times*, Nov. 6, 1961, p. 74.

and no variety of box set was permissible or even possible. For Wilder decries the box set in the 1960's as vehemently as in 1938 when *Our Town* played its first performance. In his opinion, such a set reduces drama to anecdote, conceals the universal implications of the action, and narrows the effectiveness of the play to a point where it is no longer comparable in impact to a good musical performance or art exhibition.[8]

Commenting on his plans and the first three plays to be presented in the Bleecker Street house some months before their opening on January 11, 1962, Wilder vouchsafed two important clues to the tone the series would take. First, they would be highly abstract: "I am interested in the drives that operate in society and in every man. . . . Pride, avarice and envy are in every home. I am not interested in the ephemeral—such subjects as the adulteries of dentists. I am interested in those things that repeat and repeat and repeat in the lives of the millions." From this remark and the decision to employ the sort of stage for which the box set is impractical, it was possible to foretell a return to the method of *Our Town*. But this impression was modified by the assurance that the plays would be comic: "Because we live in the twentieth century, overhung by very real anxiety, we have to use the comic spirit. . . . No statement of gravity can be equal to the gravity of the age in which we live."[9] We may expect, then, that in various ways and to varying degrees the fourteen one-acts will reflect the comic sense of life which Wilder has always been reluctant to dismiss and to which he always returns after excursions into tragedy.

Of the three plays so far presented, it can be said that they hint of a substantial legacy in store for audiences of the future. They are, however, pieces of remarkably

[8] Gelb, *loc. cit.*
[9] Gelb, *loc. cit.*

unequal merit. *Someone from Assisi*, the drama on lust from the group on the seven deadly sins, left its first audience in a muddle over its actual purpose, since the action seemed far too ethereal to correspond to popular images of lust. The two plays from the group on the ages of man, *Infancy* and *Childhood*, were more widely praised. The second of the two reminded onlookers of *Our Town* by virtue of its many notations of the difficulty of communication between parents and children and, more tellingly, because of its tranquility and depth of feeling. Largely on the strength of *Childhood*, the plays remained at the Circle in the Square into the fall, for the longest run in recent history of a bill of one-act plays in New York.[10]

It is to be hoped that Wilder will find it as easy to dismiss *Someone from Assisi* as did his audience. A dull, unmoving piece, on nearly every line it slips into the precious, poetic diction of the three-minute plays of Wilder's youth. In it appears a madwoman whose difficulties have issued from her ultimate rejection by Francis of Assisi after a youthful love affair. Now a monk, Francis is able to maintain spiritual strength only by withdrawing from all fleshly temptation. Meeting the woman again after some years when friends ask him to dinner, he is deeply moved by her state and vows to provide for her. True, he had once experienced lust and is

[10] In numbers of tickets sold, Clifford Odets's double bill of *Waiting for Lefty* and *Till the Day I Die* (168 performances, 1935) and Arthur Miller's double bill of *A Memory of Two Mondays* and *A View from the Bridge* (149 performances, 1955–1956) may possibly have done better than Wilder's triple bill (344 performances), since the Broadway houses in which they were presented are approximately three times the size of the Bleecker Street house of the Circle in the Square. Nevertheless the length of Wilder's run is most impressive in view of the relative inaccessibility of the theater and the fact that his was a bill of very short plays, whereas Odets's audience was drawn chiefly by the widely publicized *Lefty* and Miller's by *A View*, actually a work long enough to stand on its own.

now preoccupied with suppressing it, but as a theme that particular sin is so far removed from the dialogue and tone of the play that it is scarcely present at all. A faint but unintentional note of comedy creeps in as the final absurdity when Francis in penitence for his error of the deep past requests his friends to prepare his supper without the touch of saffron he usually enjoys.

The diction of *Infancy* and *Childhood* is much superior. The plays are couched in the everyday phrasing which has been the mark of Wilder's best work for the stage since the one-acts of 1931. It is their colloquial and jocular language which makes them appealing as much as the wisdom which they exhibit. They are, moreover, funny (in part), as befits drama on the first stages of life, before innocence is threatened.

Though not so much admired as *Childhood*, the first play on the ages of man is good enough to be retained in the cycle, provided a few minor roughnesses of language are pressed out. *Infancy* is an intellectual farce, a play which through laughter makes a sound point on what it is like for babies to live at the mercy of their parents. The two infants are played by grown men wearing the lace gowns and caps in which adoring mothers dress their youngest for airings in the park. To express his belief that the present alarming state of the world is due to the follies of older generations, the sexagenarian Wilder, like the angriest of young playwrights, gives heavy weight to the wisdom of the young and shows their elders to be somewhat dim-witted by contrast. Yet he does not mar the comic tone by bulking the speech of the two carriage-bound babies with adult diction. He merely adds to their monosyllables a few words of dissatisfaction with the meagerness of the information given them by their parents. They would like to hear more than the multiplication tables and the names of the boroughs of

New York City, but more they cannot get from those who tend them and supposedly love them. Thus is explained the tantrums by which children bedevil their elders. Wilder's infants go through a monumental tantrum, after which one of them, showing how much he knows of the adult world beyond what his parents have taught him, proclaims for all Central Park to hear, "I want to have a baby."

A more mellow play, *Childhood* marks a return to the Grover's Corners mood, although it is set in the present time and its scene is not a village, but a suburban community. The similarity to Wilder's great play of 1938 comes through its touching awareness of the loss of youth, as reflected in the attitude of parents who stand in awe of the fantasies of their children, and in the equally touching failure of the generations to reach each other in spirit. The three children of relatively young parents pass the early evening in a long, elaborate game based on the pretense that the parents are dead and that they themselves are therefore free to wander where they please. So gripping is their fantasy that even as they draw their mother into the game as a favorite schoolteacher they can speak as though the funeral were long over and both parents were only an imperfect memory:

> CAROLINE: ... Papa was a very fine man. And ...
> DODIE (*quickly*): He used to swear bad words.
> BILLEE (*excitedly*): All the *time*! He'd swear swearwords.
> CAROLINE: Well, maybe a little.
> DODIE: He *did*. I used to want to *die*.
> CAROLINE: Well, nobody's perfeck. (*Slower.*) He was all right, sometimes.
> DODIE: He used to laugh too loud in front of people. And he didn't give Mama enough money to buy clothes. She had to go to town in rags, in terrible old rags.

BILLEE (*always excited*): Papa'd go like this (*pumping his arms up and down in desperation*): "I haven't got it! I haven't got it! You can't squeeze blood out of a stone."

DODIE: Yes, he did.

BILLEE. And Mama'd say: "I'm ashamed to go out in the street." It was awful. And then'd he'd say, "I'll have to mortgage, that's what I'll have to do."

CAROLINE: Billee! How can you say such an awful word? Don't you ever say that again. Papa wasn't perfeck, but he would never have done a mortgage.

BILLEE: Well, that's what he said.

CAROLINE (*emphatically*): Most times Papa did his best. Everybody makes some mistakes.[11]

The play continues in this vein. With their freedom secured, the children decide to take a bus trip across America. To strengthen their sense of fantasy, they take new names: Mrs. Arizona, Miss Wilson, and Mr. Wentworth. But when they queue up to seat themselves on the chairs which will represent the bus, they find that their father, hoping to play a part in their dreams, is seated as the driver and that their mother is in line with them to buy a make-believe ticket for the trip. On the bus ride, which lasts no more than ten minutes, the father likens the cross-country trip to the voyage through life, inasmuch as both have their dangers along with their pleasant moments. This lesson is not lost on the children, who become increasingly mellow and conversational as the seconds pass. When it is all over, they appear to have a new consideration for the parents, in gratitude for their sensible, adult behavior on the journey, but in a few minutes they are off again in another dream.

Although the pathos of this little piece struck a few of the reviewers as rank sentimentality, *Childhood* does not deserve such a complaint. It has the merit of taking us

11 Wilder, "Childhood," *Atlantic*, CCVI (Nov. 1960), 80.

back to our first youth, when dissatisfaction with our parents gives way suddenly to affection, unexpectedly creating a sensation we would prefer not to know, but whose clutch we cannot elude. This is the quality of *Our Town*. The play is a little like *The Happy Journey to Trenton and Camden* also, for in addition to the bitter-sweet feeling of family love which sets the tone of that piece, it employs the device of travel through strange territory to give the occupants of the bus a sense of intimacy. Although it would be injudicious of Wilder to adopt the same tone for all fourteen plays of the series, he is wise to use it where he can. The profound sincerity of the dialogue, which is once more the language of middle-class life, gives body to what might otherwise turn into anecdote, and very thin anecdote at that.

We do not know, as of this moment, when Wilder will finish his novel and return to the dramatic cycle. For that matter, we have no guarantee from him that he will go back to it at all. But whatever appears will be welcome, for the direction of his career is itself a guarantee that while he continues to write he will invent fresh expressive forms with which to astonish his readers.

VII. For the Time Being

ALL THE PHOTOGRAPHS of Wilder, the casual snapshots and studio portraits alike, published over the four decades of his fame have this in common: they show a man who looks older than his years, whose gaze is focused intently on an object close at hand, and who is on the point of breaking into a broad smile (a few pictures of recent date record the smile in full width). Curiously obscuring his youthful delight in adventure and minimizing his comic vision, the pictures are truthful only in presenting to the beholder a strong hint of Wilder's creative intelligence— of that mind that probes into and delights in all the benign varieties of human activity. What has given him the look of age cannot be illness, for he has suffered no serious ailments, or fatigue, for his energy is endless, or overwhelming sadness, for his life has been singularly free of grief and rancor, the controversies of 1930 and 1943 notwithstanding. "I'm almost sixty and look it," he remarked in 1956. "I'm the kind of man whom timid old ladies stop on the street to ask about the nearest subway station. News vendors in university towns call me 'professor,' and hotel clerks, 'doctor.'"[1] His self-image, though revealed here in comic terms, is accurate enough; he looks to be exactly what he is: a man of authority whose position in life is the natural result of intellectual distinction. The look of age is the look of wisdom.

Seen close to, he invariably projects the sense of comedy and the infinite curiosity suppressed in the photographs, whether speaking with intimate acquaintances of many years or an interviewer come to gather in a few salable insights into his work. All who speak with him comment on his gregariousness—surely his most frequently recorded trait of character—and his wit. That he is seldom bored is equally obvious; something in the man forbids tediousness in others, or elicits from them their best conversational efforts. He is a born teacher, but one for whom the dry method of classroom instruction is impossible; at Chicago and at Harvard his way was a happy combination of informality and dramatic flair, the shortish (and later stoutish) physique marching about the room, the arms beating the air, and the fingers stabbing to punctuate an idea.[2] Along with this performance was present—and still is—his happy awareness of having got the good out of life, as though he had not only accomplished what he had set out to do but had enjoyed doing it.

If now in his sixties with plans for the novel and the cycle of short plays much on his mind he seems to be in "a sedate hurry,"[3] he is not and never has been in a blind rush to proceed in life from incident to incident, but has relished each and thoroughly lived it. Tyrone Guthrie, whose acquaintance with Wilder goes back to the early

<hr>

[1] Richard H. Goldstone, "Thornton Wilder," in *Writers at Work: The Paris Review Interviews*, ed. Malcolm Cowley (New York: Viking Press, 1958), p. 101.

[2] "An Obliging Man," *Time*, LXI (Jan. 12, 1953), 46.

[3] Flora Lewis, "Thornton Wilder at 65 Looks Ahead—and Back," New York *Times Magazine*, April 15, 1962, p. 28.

1930's, has given a little bravura sketch that highlights the qualities which many have described more abstractly:

> Wilder is learned but no pedant. I have never met anyone with so encyclopedic a knowledge of so wide a range of topics. Yet he carries this learning lightly and imparts it—the important with the trivial, the commonplace with the exceedingly bizarre—in a style and with a gusto which is all his own.
>
> The manner is confidential and quite giggly; incredibly rapid utterance, accompanied by a series of stabbing gestures and jerky curlicues executed with the forefinger, as though he were tatting an invisible and refractory wire net. He has been everywhere, has known—and knows—everyone, and is fond of a sort of name-dropping which might seem snobbish if its purpose were not obviously the further embellishment of an already ornate controversial style. "Texas Guinan and I were in a goat-carriage on Michigan Avenue . . . Bertrand Russell dipped *his* in brandy . . . Ernst Lubitsch leaned across my plate and whispered to His Holiness. . . ."[4]

We are taken back to *The Cabala*, and Wilder is a Cabalist without the neurotic stubbornness that diminishes the pleasures of wisdom and position.

The joy of living so notable a part of the private citizen Wilder is, we know, the theme of Wilder the writer. As we have seen, in one guise or another, and sometimes as in *The Ides of March* even a melancholy guise, it is present in every play and novel, regardless of the setting— Old World or New, present or past—and regardless of the presentational method—straightforward or epistolary narrative, tragedy or farce, the bare stage or the box set. In *The Cabala, The Bridge of San Luis Rey*, and *Heaven's My Destination*, Wilder has used his theme to show the

[4] Tyrone Guthrie, *A Life in the Theatre* (New York: McGraw-Hill, 1959), p. 232.

problem of the neurotic who cannot bring to an end that absorption with self which so deprives him of pleasure in the world around him that he cannot be said truly to have lived at all. Perverse satisfaction with ugliness, grief, and loneliness gives order to the existence of the characters of these novels, but at the same time it ossifies their emotional life. The conservatism of the Greek elders in *The Woman of Andros* and the assassins of *The Ides of March* is a similar affliction, stunting the growth of Simo's spirit, blinding the Pulchers, Brutus, and Cassius to the value of Caesar's experiments, and ultimately bringing disaster to all.

The cry of Emily in the last act of *Our Town* is Wilder's most explicit statement of the theme, and the (literally) millions of persons who have viewed the play as originally written for the stage or in the screen or television versions have understood it along with the heroine. But it is memorably presented in *The Matchmaker* and *The Skin of Our Teeth* also. Through the contrast between Dolly Levi and Horace Vandergelder we are given to understand the dreariness of the closed-in personality, and in the antics of the clerks we witness the marvel of the liberation of the spirit. Among Wilder's major works *The Skin of Our Teeth* presents the theme in its most abstract, complex form, but presents it forcefully nevertheless. The bright and the dark aspects of life are on view in every act, and the dark as shown in the personality of Henry-Cain, man against himself, is to be preserved and tolerated because of the challenge it delivers which forces man for his own protection to enlarge whatever is valuable in himself. This firm conviction that life is a process worthy of man's effort underlies the new cycle of plays, in seven of which Wilder will describe man's growing awareness of the world from infancy on, and in the seven others on sin in which he will describe the deterrents to his development.

The theme, we have seen, is effective in both tragedy and comedy. Wilder, however, has written tragedy less frequently than comedy and far more tentatively, so that in several of the major works we may not immediately ascertain which of the two modes we are confronting. *The Bridge of San Luis Rey* must be classed as tragedy if for no other reason than that it terminates with the death of its protagonists. But these unfortunate characters do not die until they have been purged of their dangerously debilitating fixations, and, once that step is over, proceed to the reward of peace. The action of *Our Town* is tragic, to be sure, but, deeply moving though the play is, it is held back a little by the enlargement of Emily into an allegorical figure; in connection with this process we must remember that Wilder authorized the happy ending of the film on the consideration that the realism of the screen would render the death of Emily too cruel for the audience. Julius Caesar in *The Ides of March* moves far more certainly into unrelieved tragedy than the protagonists of any of the other works, for his fall, determined by the absurdity of those surrounding him and by his own inability to compromise, is not softened by the suggestion that in death he will achieve contentment or any other form of reward. But Wilder has not returned to stark tragedy since 1948 and gives no hint that he intends to do so; his version of the Alcestis story is more moving than is the version of Euripides, but it ends triumphantly in the heroine's release from slavery and the fulfillment of her prayer for knowledge of the existence of the gods.

As for the rest of the major works, not to mention the short plays of the 1930's and 1960's, they are comic treatments of the theme, even if the characters have not progressed from neurotic shortsightedness to healthy, panoramic vision. The cabalistic society of twentieth-century Rome may be breaking up at the close of Wilder's first novel, but that the old power should fade is healthy, not tragic, for it has not proved of great value, and Samuele learns from the ghost of Virgil that he must found a new city on principles other than the Cabalists'. George Brush's own affairs are in the same deplorable state at the close of *Heaven's My Destination* that we observe at its opening, and the prospect of happiness for him in this life is dim indeed. But he speeds along his own special route in life toward the heaven of which he is so certain, and Wilder makes not the slightest suggestion that George may be grandly deceived as to its existence. Setting *The Matchmaker* to one side, no other work of Wilder's is so obviously comic as *The Skin of Our Teeth*, despite its glacier, its flood, and its fires of war. It may be more correct to say that these catastrophes provide the comic conflict—that because of them the play is comic—for they are the threats which the human race must avert in its determination to keep moving on, just as the ardent lover in a bedroom farce must bluff a menacing husband not once but again and again on his unexpected appearances at the scene of a tryst.

Because they are conceived as comedies, such works as *The Cabala, Heaven's My Destination*, and *The Skin of Our Teeth* have seemed to some of Wilder's readers to fail to grant close attention to serious subjects or to deny them the full measure of their seriousness—in other words, to lack depth. Because such works as *The Bridge of San Luis Rey, Our Town*, and the recent *Childhood* describe relationships without obvious recourse to psychoanalytic doctrine or economic determinism, some readers have also charged him with heart-on-sleeve sentimentality. But unfavorable or friendly, the criticism of his work has been niggardly; it would be difficult to make up a book-length anthology of intelligent essays on his fiction and drama such as those which have recently appeared on the work of many of his contemporaries. Nor has he figured in the standard histories of American literature beyond a few grudging sentences. Although it is a serious complaint to level against the major critics of his time, one reason for the relative disinterest in his work may lie in his popularity with general readers and playgoers. The public can be right, however, and in the case of Wilder its judgment is sound. The eyes behind the horn-rimmed spectacles have probed into the values of life, and under the colloquial language which he has employed for its appeal to the minds of Americans can be heard an urgent call to reason. The small number of carefully made works which he has issued over four decades have made their point, and it is doubtful that any of them save *The Cabala* and *The Woman of Andros* will drop into oblivion. *Our Town*, in all likelihood the most widely produced play in the entire history of American drama, and *The Skin of Our Teeth* have deserved the prizes bestowed on them by the Pulitzer committee as surely as any of the other plays granted the same award; and if *The Bridge of San Luis Rey* is not the best novel to have won the Pulitzer Prize, Wilder's five novels as a group have justly earned the Gold Medal for fiction given to him by the American Academy of Arts and Letters in 1952.

Being a conscientious craftsman, Wilder has grown steadily in strength and taste. If the hyperliterary style of the first three novels tempers our enjoyment, we need not be embarrassed by the fact, but at the same time we should not use it as an excuse for damning the later works, where the language comes down to the level of the matters under discussion. With the one-act plays of 1931 he proved the sharpness of his ear, and of all the subsequent works only *Someone from Assisi* falls back into the vapid early style. When he finds the correct form for the accommodation of his latest insight into the springs of action, as he has done with *Heaven's My Destination*, *Our Town*, and *The Skin of Our Teeth*, it is not through happy accident, obviously enough, but through earnest study and trial. We would be unfair to think of him as only an experimenter, despite the variety of his means of expression as evident particularly in the plays, since each work is a finished product. The experiments are the drafts which lead up to the finished pieces, and drafts, as he has said, go into the wastebasket. It is true that his inherent didacticism and pleasure in learning marred the surface of his first two novels to the extent that a few of their paragraphs read rather more like lists of the cultural phenomena of Rome and Lima than like fiction; these might have landed in the wastebasket with some benefit to the novels. But the habit of name- or title-dropping, however much it may still affect his conversation, is no longer a threat to his literary style. The bookishness complained of by critics of *The Skin of Our Teeth* is a quite different concern from the tedious catalogues of composers and authors in the early fiction and far more defensible, for it is by remembering the monuments to its intelligence created by philosophers, playwrights, and novelists that the human race strengthens itself to continue on its difficult course. Cavils against *The Ides of March* on the ground that it also exudes the air of the classroom may be dismissed routinely with the answer that the reader who finds it too learned for his taste may turn to something else, since no writer is under obligation to entertain all the people all the time.

In respect to his entire list of works, however, Wilder has managed to entertain all the people on one occasion or another, and to show sympathy for all. The undergraduate snobbery of *The Cabala* gave way once the book was published to a vision which includes the gamut of economic classes and levels of intelligence. Uncle Pio is no less impressive to him than is the Marquesa, and the unfortunate wards of Chrysis no less important than the elegant courtesan herself. The middle-class businessmen and commercial travelers of *Heaven's My Destination* are treated with no trace of condescension for all their boobery; moreover, those among them who are in trouble, like the suicidal Dick Roberts, are described with such roundness as to suggest that Wilder had drawn them from live originals close to himself. In *Our Town* the sympathy of the audience is as firmly drawn toward the not-so-bright George, especially in his grief, as toward the more intelligent Emily, and as the play progresses we are made to understand that our world includes an infinite variety of well-intentioned creatures from newsboys to learned professors of geology, all of whom deserve our respectful attention.

The broadening range of the novels and plays is a reflection of the broadening process constantly at work within Wilder's own personality, the happy result of continued inquiry into new systems of philosophy, along with a steady enthusiasm for new experiences, as evident in his delight in travel. It was no easy matter for him to shake off the Calvinism handed down to him, or clamped around him, by his father. The effort it cost him is apparent in the delineation of Samuele and the description of that young American's struggle to cope with the outlook of Roman society. It is clearer still in the picture of George Brush in battle with the world. But under pressure of his will to get on into life, the constraints of Calvinism loosened, and it is obvious from the record of his travels and additions to his circle of friends that well before 1935, when he published the chronicle of Brush, Wilder had found very deep enjoyment in his personal fame and had even come so far along the broad path of permissiveness followed by most of mankind that he could look back with some slight amusement on the memory of his youthful austerity.

In due course Wilder also turned from humanism, though it is doubtful that even today the break is complete, since he has never attempted a naturalistic play or novel and has had nothing to say about naturalism in his critical writing. Still, the plays of 1931 with their focus upon inelegant middle-class manners reveal that he has made a considerable descent from the grand pinnacles inhabited by Babbitt and More. Immediately after the Second World War he moved so far from the influences of his formative years that he could look tolerantly on the atheistic philosophy of Sartre, and though he could not renounce a belief in the existence of God, he accepted Sartre's view that life takes form for individual man only as he adjusts to its hardships and willingly accepts impossible tasks if to do so is to fulfill his capacity for living. These shifts and adjustments have strengthened his work by removing from it the mawkish prettiness that in part characterizes the early novels. That he responded to the unorthodox thought of Gertrude Stein is additional evidence of his growth, since nothing could be farther removed from the regularity of his academic training. It is clear from the postwar lectures in which he explores the idea of the American as the possessor of a "planetary mind" that this influence is still active.[5]

More certainly than for his contemporaries of comparable reputation it can be claimed for Wilder that he is the possessor of such a mind. Although he has successfully portrayed the American character in drama and fiction, he has never pursued so narrow a vein of national interest

[5] See the Charles Eliot Norton lectures and excerpts from Wilder's 1951 commencement address at Harvard, *Harvard Alumni Magazine*, LIII (July 17, 1951), 779–781. See also "World Literature and the Modern Mind," in *Goethe and the Modern Age*, ed. Arnold Bergstraesser (Chicago: Henry Regnery, 1950), pp. 213–224.

that his works were closed to audiences abroad. As often as not he has directed his gaze to other continents and has recorded images that have shown Americans how vast is the common experience of all people. He has seized upon personal issues at once great and small—those which, to take up a phrase from *The Bridge of San Luis Rey*, are the notation of the heart. The political and sociological issues of an age may be resolved, leaving the novels and plays devoted to them nothing more than material for archivists. But Wilder has given full treatment to the problems that occur with never-ending urgency in the life of each member of the race.

A Bibliographical Note

THE FOLLOWING IS a chronological listing of the books by Wilder quoted or cited in the text. Unless otherwise indicated, all are first editions.

THE CABALA. New York: Albert & Charles Boni, 1926.

THE BRIDGE OF SAN LUIS REY. New York: Albert & Charles Boni, 1927.

THE ANGEL THAT TROUBLED THE WATERS AND OTHER PLAYS. New York: Coward-McCann, 1928.

THE WOMAN OF ANDROS. New York: Albert & Charles Boni, 1930.

THE LONG CHRISTMAS DINNER AND OTHER PLAYS IN ONE ACT. New York: Coward-McCann; New Haven: Yale University Press, 1931.

HEAVEN'S MY DESTINATION. New York: Harper & Brothers, 1935. First American edition; preceded by English edition.

OUR TOWN. New York: Coward-McCann [1938].

THE MERCHANT OF YONKERS. New York: Harper & Brothers, 1939.

THE SKIN OF OUR TEETH. New York: Harper & Brothers, 1942.

OUR CENTURY, N.p.: Century Association, 1947.

THE IDES OF MARCH. New York: Harper & Brothers [1948].

THREE PLAYS. New York: Harper & Brothers [1957]. Includes *Our Town*, *The Skin of Our Teeth*, and *The Matchmaker*—first publication of the last-named.

DIE ALKESTIADE, trans. Herberth E. Herlitschka. Frankfurt am Main and Hamburg, 1960.

The following five major contributions to periodicals to date have not been gathered into books. The first three are from Wilder's Charles Eliot Norton lectures of 1950–1951.

"Toward an American Language." *Atlantic*, CXC (July 1952). 29–37.

"The American Loneliness." *Atlantic*, CXC (Aug. 1952). 65–69.

"Emily Dickinson." *Atlantic*, CXC (Nov. 1952). 43–48.

"The Drunken Sisters." *Atlantic*, CC (Nov. 1957). 92–95.

"Childhood." *Atlantic*, CCVI (Nov. 1960). 78–84.

For a list of all Wilder's publications through 1958, complete except for pieces written for the New York *Times*, see J. M. Edelstein, *A Bibliographical Checklist of the Writings of Thornton Wilder* (New Haven: Yale University Library, 1959).

The reader who wishes to study in detail the judgments passed on Wilder's writing over the decades should consult Heinz Kosok's invaluable "Thornton Wilder: A Bibliography of Criticism," *Twentieth Century Literature*, IX (1963), 93–100. Of special interest by virtue of their length are the three books on Wilder which have preceded the study at hand: Rex Burbank, *Thornton Wilder*, New York: Twayne Publishers, 1961; Helmut Papajewski, *Thornton Wilder*, Frankfurt am Main and Bonn: Athenäum Verlag, 1961; Herman Stresau, *Thornton Wilder*, Berlin: Colloquium Verlag, 1963 (not mentioned by Kosok). For impressions of Wilder the man, especially to be recommended are Edith J. R. Isaacs, "Thornton Wilder in Person," *Theatre Arts*, XXVII (1943), 21–30; Glenway Wescott, *Images of Truth*, New York: Harper & Row, 1962; and Edmund Wilson, *The Shores of Light*, New York: Farrar, Straus and Young, 1952. Wilder's own appraisal of his life and work is recorded in his Paris interview with Richard H. Goldstone, reprinted in *Writers at Work*, ed. Malcolm Cowley, New York: Viking Press, 1958. In addition to this interview and the relevant portions of the books by Wescott and Wilson, the list of helpful essays on Wilder's fiction and drama is, in the present writer's opinion, limited to eight. They are as follows:

CORRIGAN, ROBERT W. "Thornton Wilder and the Tragic Sense of Life." *Educational Theatre Journal*, XIII (1961). 167–173.

COWLEY, MALCOLM. Introduction. *A Thornton Wilder Trio*. New York: Criterion Books, 1956.

FERGUSSON, FRANCIS. "Three Allegorists: Brecht, Wilder and Eliot." *Sewanee Review*, LXIV (1956), 544–573; reprinted in Fergusson, *The Human Image in Dramatic Literature*. New York: Doubleday Anchor Books, 1957. Pp. 41–71.

FIREBAUGH, JOSEPH. "The Humanism of Thornton Wilder." *Pacific Spectator*, IV (1950). 426–438.

FULLER, EDMUND. "Thornton Wilder: 'The Notation of the Heart.'" *American Scholar*, XXVIII (1959). 210–217.

HEWITT, BARNARD. "Thornton Wilder Says 'Yes.'" *Tulane Drama Review*, IV (Dec. 1959). 110–120.

McCARTHY, MARY. "Class Angles and a Wilder Classic." *Sights and Spectacles*. New York: Farrar, Straus and Cudahy, 1956. Pp. 21–29.

———. "The Skin of Our Teeth." *Sights and Spectacles*. New York: Farrar, Straus and Cudahy, 1956. Pp. 53–56.

Acknowledgment

I GRATEFULLY ACKNOWLEDGE permission to quote from the following copyrighted works:

To Mr. Thornton Wilder for permission to quote from *The Cabala, The Bridge of San Luis Rey, The Angel That Troubled the Waters, The Woman of Andros,* "Noting the Nature of Farce," "Our Town—From Stage to Screen," "James Joyce (1882–1941)," "Some Thoughts on Play-writing," and an undated letter to Paul Friedman.

To Harper & Row for permission to quote from Thornton Wilder, *The Long Christmas Dinner, Heaven's My Destination, Our Town, The Skin of Our Teeth, The Ides of March,* and *Three Plays.*

To the *Atlantic* for permission to quote from Thornton Wilder, "Childhood."

To Alfred A. Knopf for permission to quote from *The Flowers of Friendship: Letters to Gertrude Stein,* ed. Donald Gallup.

To McGraw-Hill for permission to quote from Tyrone Guthrie, *A Life in the Theatre.*

To the Viking Press for permission to quote from Alexander Woollcott, *Letters,* ed. Beatrice Kaufman and

Joseph Hennessey; and to the Viking Press and the *Paris Review* for permission to quote from Richard H. Goldstone, "Thornton Wilder," in *Writers at Work: The Paris Review Interviews*, ed. Malcolm Cowley.

To the *Saturday Review* for permission to quote from Ross Parmenter, "Novelist into Playwright."

To *Time* for permission to quote from "An Obliging Man."

To the New York *Times* for permission to quote from Arthur Gelb, "Thornton Wilder, 63, Sums Up Life and Art," and from "Wilder to Relax in Desert Two Years" and "Hideaway in Italy Chosen by Wilder."

M.G.

Index